THE COMPLETE GUIDE TO

HIRING A LITERARY AGENT:

Everything You Need to Know to Become Successfully Published

By Laura Cross

The Complete Guide to Hiring a Literary Agent: Everything You Need to Know to Become Successfully Published

Library of Congress Cataloging-in-Publication Data

Cross, Laura, 1969-
  The complete guide to hiring a literary agent : everything you need to know to become successfully published / by Laura Cross.
       p. cm.
  Includes bibliographical references and index.
  ISBN-13: 978-1-60138-403-4 (alk. paper)
  ISBN-10: 1-60138-403-3 (alk. paper)
  1. Authorship--Marketing--Handbooks, manuals, etc. 2. Authors and publishers--Handbooks, manuals, etc. 3. Literary agents. I. Title.
  PN161.C76 2010
  070.5'2--dc22
                              2009048427

PROJECT MANAGER: Kim Fulscher • EDITORIAL INTERN: Amber McDonald
PRE-PRESS & PRODUCTION DESIGN: Holly Marie Gibbs
COVER DESIGN & INTERIOR LAYOUT: Meg Buchner • meg@megbuchner.com
BACK COVER DESIGN: Jackie Miller • millerjackiej@gmail.com

Printed on Recycled Paper

Printed in the United States

We recently lost our beloved pet "Bear," who was not only our best and dearest friend but also the "Vice President of Sunshine" here at Atlantic Publishing. He did not receive a salary but worked tirelessly 24 hours a day to please his parents. Bear was a rescue dog that turned around and showered myself, my wife, Sherri, his  grandparents Jean, Bob, and Nancy, and every person and animal he met (maybe not rabbits) with friendship and love. He made a lot of people smile every day.

We wanted you to know that a portion of the profits of this book will be donated to The Humane Society of the United States. *–Douglas & Sherri Brown*

The human-animal bond is as old as human history. We cherish our animal companions for their unconditional affection and acceptance. We feel a thrill when we glimpse wild creatures in their natural habitat or in our own backyard.

Unfortunately, the human-animal bond has at times been weakened. Humans have exploited some animal species to the point of extinction.

The Humane Society of the United States makes a difference in the lives of animals here at home and worldwide. The HSUS is dedicated to creating a world where our relationship with animals is guided by compassion. We seek a truly humane society in which animals are respected for their intrinsic value, and where the human-animal bond is strong.

Want to help animals? We have plenty of suggestions. Adopt a pet from a local shelter, join The Humane Society and be a part of our work to help companion animals and wildlife. You will be funding our educational, legislative, investigative and outreach projects in the U.S. and across the globe.

Or perhaps you'd like to make a memorial donation in honor of a pet, friend or relative? You can through our Kindred Spirits program. And if you'd like to contribute in a more structured way, our Planned Giving Office has suggestions about estate planning, annuities, and even gifts of stock that avoid capital gains taxes.

Maybe you have land that you would like to preserve as a lasting habitat for wildlife. Our Wildlife Land Trust can help you. Perhaps the land you want to share is a backyard— that's enough. Our Urban Wildlife Sanctuary Program will show you how to create a habitat for your wild neighbors.

So you see, it's easy to help animals. And The HSUS is here to help.

2100 L Street NW • Washington, DC 20037 • 202-452-1100
www.hsus.org

Table of Contents

FOREWORD   **9**

INTRODUCTION   **11**

SECTION 1: PREPARING TO ACQUIRE
A LITERARY AGENT   **13**

CHAPTER 1: WHY YOU NEED AN AGENT   **15**

What Literary Agents Do 15
The Publishing Industry...16
The Benefits of a Literary Agent...20
How To Know When You Are Ready for an Agent............................23

CHAPTER 2: UNDERSTANDING THE MARKET   **27**

What Agents Look For 27
Publishing Trends and Seasons 30
Understanding Your Genre..33

CHAPTER 3: ESTABLISHING YOUR AUTHOR PLATFORM AND BUILDING CREDENTIALS 45

Establishing a Platform 46
Building Credentials 50

CHAPTER 4: FINDING AND SELECTING AN AGENT 53

How to Find Agents 53
Researching Agents...62
Creating an Agent File...65

SECTION 2: SUBMITTING THE PITCH 67

CHAPTER 5: THE PITCH PACKAGE 69

Understanding the Elements of the Pitch Package 70
Approaching Agents 71
The Submission Process 72
Getting to "Yes"...77

CHAPTER 6: CRAFTING THE QUERY LETTER 81

Components of the Query Letter 81
Query Formatting Rules...84
12 Tips for Writing an Effective Nonfiction Query Letter 85
Eight Tips For Creating An Effective Fiction Query Letter................89
Do's and Don'ts of Query Letter Writing..90

CHAPTER 7: CREATING THE BOOK PROPOSAL 95

The Purpose of a Book Proposal...95
The Components Of A Book Proposal..96
Formatting and Packaging Your Book Proposal 104
The Top Ten Reasons Book Proposals Are Rejected 106

CHAPTER 8: WRITING THE SYNOPSIS   109

What An Agent Looks For In A Synopsis 109
How To Write an Effective Synopsis 110
Formatting the Synopsis 113

CHAPTER 9: PREPARING AND POLISHING THE MANUSCRIPT   117

Editing and Proofreading 117
Writing Critique Groups and Beta Readers 119
Story Checklists 120
The Top Five Reasons a Manuscript is Rejected 122
Formatting Your Manuscript 122

SECTION 3: HIRING A LITERARY AGENT   129

CHAPTER 10: WAITING FOR A RESPONSE   131

Use Your Time Wisely 131
When to Follow Up 133
Learning From Rejection 134
Tips For Submitting Additional Requested Material 136

CHAPTER 11: EVALUATING AN AGENT'S OFFER   141

Questions to Ask the Agent You May Hire 141
Avoiding Scams and Assuring Credibility 147
The Author-Agent Agreement 149

CHAPTER 12: GETTING THE BOOK DEAL   155

Selling the Book 155
The Publishing Contract 159
Maintaining a Successful Working Relationship with Your Agent 163
When To Consider Ending The Author-Agent Partnership 166

APPENDIX I: LITERARY AGENTS LOOKING FOR NEW WRITERS 173

APPENDIX II: NATIONAL WRITER'S ORGANIZATIONS 183

APPENDIX III: NATIONAL WRITER'S CONFERENCES 185

APPENDIX IV: GENRE DEFINITIONS 187

APPENDIX V: THE SIX LARGE PUBLISHING HOUSES AND THEIR IMPRINTS 195

APPENDIX VI: GLOSSARY OF TERMS 201

APPENDIX VII: SUCCESSFUL QUERY LETTERS AND SYNOPSES 205

Successful Query Letter: Narrative Nonfiction 205
Successful Query Letter: Memoir 207
Successful Query Letter: Nonfiction Anthology..............................208
Successful Query Letter: How-To (Practical) Nonfiction 210
Successful Query Letter: Urban Fantasy...212
Successful Query Letter: Cozy Mystery 213
Successful Query Letter: Christian Literary Fiction 214
Successful Query Letter: Historical Children's Fiction 215
Successful Query Letter: Humorous Paranormal 216
Successful Query Letter: Erotic Romance..217
Successful Synopsis: Modern Romance Novel 218
Successful Synopsis: Chick-Lit Novel 226
Successful Synopsis: Mystery Novel...232
Successful Synopsis: Young Adult Novel..237

APPENDIX VIII: SAMPLE FORMATTED MANUSCRIPT PAGES — 241

Title Page 241
Table of Contents Page...242
First Page of Chapter Format................................243
Formatting for Subsequent Chapter Pages 244

APPENDIX IX: SUCCESSFUL BOOK PROPOSAL — 245

APPENDIX X: SAMPLE AUTHOR/AGENT CONTRACT — 267

APPENDIX XI: SAMPLE REVISED PAGES — 279

Original Draft 279
Revised Draft 280

BIBLIOGRAPHY — 283

AUTHOR BIOGRAPHY — 284

INDEX — 285

Foreword

I have enough experience to know within one week of working with an author if he or she will succeed in obtaining a book deal. Success is achieved through preparation and hard work. Becoming a published author requires marketing and promotion. Most writers do not market and promote themselves. Why? Because it is hard work — it is research, it is presenting yourself as valuable, it is sales, it is pitch, and it is finding a literary agent. It takes time and effort to do these tasks.

The craft of writing is a process anyone can eventually learn. Becoming successfully published is up to you. You may have mastered the craft, learned how to create a character, and can tell a story that will pull readers' heartstrings and make them weep. Or perhaps you are a nonfiction writer who is an expert in your field and have a true story to tell or a method to share that will change someone's life. You have the craft; now you need to commit to the marketing and promotion.

What exactly is marketing and promotion? In my capacity with helping writers become published authors, I can say that it is: to learn the publishing business, mastermind a platform for yourself, and persuade a literary agent with your perfected story in order to acquire representation. It is a long road, but one that is easily traveled if you have the right resources and the time to implement them. Laura Cross' book, *The Complete Guide to Hiring a Literary Agent: Everything you Need to Know to Become Successfully Published,* is an illuminated pathway for this feat. Cross has done most of the research for you. Like the story of Theseus and the Minotaur, Cross has left a string that leads you through the dark maze of writing and publishing and back again. All the information is here — you just have to plot it out for yourself and use it.

Cross explains how the business works, defines book categories and terminology, and gives you a crash course on what agents can do, what they want, and where to find representation. She walks you through marketing: How to create a platform, how to select agents, and how to create pitches and queries. Cross explains how to compile a nonfiction book proposal and synopsis, along with information on contracts and how a book sells. She includes advice from several published authors and what worked for them, along with advice from successful literary agents. Cross has written in a voice that is instructive, encouraging, and inspirational. In *The Complete Guide to Hiring a Literary Agent,* writers who pen novels and nonfiction alike will find valuable information to help them on their journey ro becoming a career author.

*Andrea Campbell is the author of 12 nonfiction books on a variety of topics including forensic science, criminal law, and entertaining. She is currently writing a histori-cal-biography that will be released in June 2010 through Overlook Press. Andrea is currently teaching two e-courses: "Publish That Book: How to Write a Nonfiction Book Proposal That Sells," and "The Gatekeepers: All About Agents and Editors — Getting Them, Working with Them, and Growing as a Career Author," which are offered through the WOW! Women on Writing Web site at **www.wow-womenonwriting. com**. You can also sign up for Andrea's "Soups On," a bi-monthly author's e-newsletter for information about the book industry, interviews with experts about books and publishing, and other tips for promotion and marketing. Just send an e-mail to: andreacampbell@hughes.net and put "Newsletter" in the subject line.*

Introduction

ongratulations. You have completed your fiction manuscript and are ready to have your masterpiece published. Or perhaps you have a nonfiction book idea that is sure to be the next best seller. All you need now is to land the book deal.

A literary agent helps you do just that. Agents review thousands of queries each year searching for talented writers and material to present to publishers. Literary agents sell between 80 and 90 percent of books to publishers. The other 10 to 20 percent are pitched and sold to the publisher directly by the writer. You have a much better chance of getting a book deal when you have an agent representing you to publishers.

Well-known writers, such as Stephen King, J.K. Rowling, John Grisham, Jodi Picoult, Clive Cussler, James Patterson, Patricia Cornwell, Stephanie Meyer, and Dean Koontz all use literary agents to sell their books. Acquiring an agent can be easy. All you need to do is write a compelling and marketable manuscript or saleable book idea, and follow the literary agency's submission guidelines to be considered for representation.

This book will teach you how to:

- Establish your author platform

- Protect yourself from scams

- Select an agent that is right for you

- Evaluate and understand agency contracts

- Write a winning synopsis

- Craft a query letter

- Prepare a book proposal

- Put together an effective pitch package to attract an agent

- Find a literary agent

- Polish and package your manuscript

- Maintain a positive working relationship with your agent

Throughout the book, you will find step-by-step instructions on how to complete the necessary tasks along with expert tips from reputable agents. In each chapter, "How I Acquired My Agent" sections showcases an author who successfully hired a literary agent and reveals the techniques used to acquire the agent.

Section I covers the planning, preparation, and research necessary for acquiring a literary agent. Section II shows you how to create all the essential elements of a pitch package, including the query letter, synopsis, book proposal, and polished manuscript, and how to successfully submit your work for consideration. Section III leads you along the final path of your journey, to acquiring an agent and becoming a published author, by giving you tips on how to evaluate an offer and work in harmony with your agent to sell your book.

SECTION 1:
Preparing To Acquire A Literary Agent

Why You Need an Agent

Literary agents are experienced and knowledgeable about the publishing industry. They handle the business responsibilities and aspects of selling your book, and offer many benefits for writers who want to become successful, traditionally published authors.

WHAT LITERARY AGENTS DO

For unpublished writers, the book industry can be a competitive and confusing marketplace. A literary agent can help you navigate the landscape and get your foot in the door at a publishing house. Agents are always searching for talented writers. Like matchmakers, they bring authors (the sellers) and publishers (the buyers) together.

A literary agent acts as an author's representative. The agent's job is to find a publishing house to buy your manuscript or book idea and negotiate the contract and subsidiary rights on your behalf.

A typical day in the life of a literary agent may include:

- Reviewing query letters to acquire new writers

- Corresponding with current author-clients

- Pre-selling books

- Reading manuscripts and book proposals

- Discussing needed edits and rewrites with authors

- Explaining editorial responses and contract details

- Meeting with editors

- Following up on submissions to publishers

- Handling requests for subsidiary rights

- Attending industry conferences

- Keeping current with trade magazines and literary journals

- Tracking clients' book promotion campaigns

Before joining in partnership, let us explore the potential buyer — the publishing industry.

THE PUBLISHING INDUSTRY

As readers' lifestyles change and new technologies emerge, the publishing industry continues to expand and shift. Today, there are numerous options for publishing your book: from traditional commercial publishing with a large or mid-size publishing house to small or regional publishers, or even self-publishing, print-on-demand, and digital publishing.

The diverse publishing industry is made up of:

- Six large publishers:

  1. Random House™

  2. Simon & Schuster™

  3. HarperCollins™

4. Penguin Group

5. Harlequin Enterprises

6. Holtzbrinck Publishers

- 400 mid-size publishers (such as Publish America, Inc.)

- 100 university presses (like Stanford University Press)

- 85,000 small and self-publishing companies (for instance, Archipelago Books[SM] and Dog Ear Publishing Press)

How traditional publishing works

For fiction books or narrative nonfiction work, a literary agent will submit your complete manuscript to an editor for consideration. For nonfiction books, the agent will provide a book proposal and sample chapters. The manuscript or book proposal is analyzed by an editorial review committee, which may consist of editors, production staff, sales representatives, in-house publicists, and even the publisher or owner herself. If a publishing company decides your manuscript is compelling or your idea is viable, they will offer you a contract and an advance against future book sales.

Approximately 80 percent of all published books fail to earn back the advance given to the authors, and with the cost to produce an average hardcover book escalating upward of $50,000, publishers consider several factors before committing to develop a book:

- The quality of your writing

- If your idea or novel is marketable

- Your ability to promote and publicize the book

- If the book will be timely when published

- How large the audience is for the book

- If the book has other sales potential, such as film rights

- If your book could be a series or produce spin-offs

- If you can acquire cover quotes and a foreword

- Potential distribution channels

- How many other similar books are on the market

- If major bookstores will stock it

Fast Facts	
• 85 percent of new titles published each year are nonfiction. • 15 percent of new titles published each year are fiction. • First-time authors write 75 percent of the new nonfiction books published each year. • According to the Association of American Publishers, the publishing industry netted $25 billion in book sales in 2007.	• 85 percent of a publisher's sales come from Barnes & Noble[SM], Amazon.com[SM], Borders, and Ingram[SM]. • *Publishers Weekly* magazine reports that 172,000 new book titles and editions were published in 2005. • According to the Author's Guild, a successful fiction book sells 5,000 copies and a successful nonfiction book sells 7,500 copies.

After a traditional publisher has purchased your book, they will:

- **Take editorial control of the content.** The editor works with the author to prepare the book for publication. Substantive editing is done to ensure the content is arranged appropriately for clarity and flow. Copy editing is performed to correct any errors in formatting, punctuation, spelling, grammar, word tense and usage, and syntax. The text is also checked for copyrights, trademarks, permissions, citations, and libel. The editor will also register the copyright and obtain an ISBN (International Standard Book Number) and Library of Congress Control Number.

- **Design the book cover and sales copy.** The graphic department will prepare the artwork, lay out the cover elements, and select the typefaces.

The marketing department writes the sales copy and selects testimonials and review quotes for inclusion on the back cover and dust-jacket flaps.

- **Prepare the book for printing.** The art department designs the interior layout, typesets the text, and creates the necessary graphics, such as charts, maps, and illustrations. A galley is prepared for final review and proofing.

- **Print the book.** This process involves selecting and ordering the paper, scheduling the press, making the plates, folding and trimming the printed press sheets, and sewing or gluing them into the book's spine.

- **Prepare promotional material.** The marketing staff designs and distributes sales aids like posters, signs, fliers, and bookmarks. They also write cover letters to book reviewers and create advertising copy.

- **Market the book.** Copies of the book are sent to reviewers, advertising space is secured in magazines and online, book tours and media interviews may be organized, and catalogs are created to pre-sell the book to book-dealers.

- **Handle distribution.** Fulfill orders to major dealers, stores, and libraries.

- **Store returns.** An average of 20 to 30 percent of books shipped to dealers are returned to publishers who then store the books in warehouses. Returned books are usually sold at a discount.

Self-publishing, print-on-demand, and digital publishing

Some authors choose to forego traditional commercial publishing and self-publish their books. The advantages of self-publishing or print-on-demand (POD) are (1) the author retains complete control of all aspects of the publishing process, (2) the author retains all rights and full ownership of the book, and (3) the writer keeps all proceeds from the sales of the book. The disadvantages of self-publishing should be carefully considered before selecting this publishing option:

- High cost for printing each book (some self-publish printers charge as much as $10 per book, plus set-up fees).

- The author is responsible for all marketing and distribution.

- Most bookstores will not carry self-published books.

- The author is responsible for all expenses associated with producing a book: typesetting, indexing, book cover design, editing, proofreading, and printing.

- The author is responsible for obtaining an ISBN, UPC Bar Code, Library of Congress Control Number, and copyright registration.

- Research indicates that 85 percent of self-published books sell fewer than 200 copies.

- Mainstream media, such as *Publishers Weekly* magazine, do not review self-published books.

- Self-published authors have less credibility than traditionally published writers.

- The author is responsible for storing the product and accepting returns.

Digital books, such as those available from Amazon.com℠ as a Kindle book or e-books offered as downloadable PDF files from an author's Web site or an e-book publisher, require no printing or distribution investment. However, digital books sell far fewer copies than print books, on average a self-published book sells fewer than 200 copies while a traditionally published book sells an average of 10,000 copies.

THE BENEFITS OF A LITERARY AGENT

With all these publishing options, why not simply bypass the literary agent and approach publishers directly with your manuscript or book idea? Acquiring a literary agent as your representative provides many benefits, which include:

- **An agent understands which editors would be interested in your work.** Agents continually cultivate relationships with publishing house editors. They know which editors will be most interested in your genre, platform, and writing style based on their tastes and needs. They will submit your work to the appropriate publishers, the right imprints, the maximum number of imprints, and the correct people within those imprints — increasing your chances of being published.

- **Agents are aware of changes in the industry.** The publishing industry is constantly changing. An agent stays aware of shifts in new media and markets to better navigate the obstacles and opportunities for first-time authors.

- **Editors prefer agent submissions.** Agents have more influence with a publisher than an unknown writer does. If an agent has pre-screened the material and is willing to represent an author's work, an editor considers it more worthy than if it is submitted directly by a writer.

- **Agents ensure your manuscript is read.** Most large publishing houses only accept submissions from agents. An agent will work with you to make sure your material is as strong as it can be before submitting it for consideration.

- **An agent can ensure a better deal and create a bidding war.** Agents will get your manuscript or book proposal seen by the maximum number of publishers. If multiple publishers are interested in the project, a powerful agent can coordinate a bidding war. Without an agent you will not know what other publishers may offer.

- **Agents understand publishing contracts and are experienced negotiators.** Publishing contracts are written for the benefit of the publishing house, not the author. An agent is familiar with contractual language and can negotiate a contract that is beneficial to the author, ensuring larger advances and royalties and changing smaller contract points to your favor. A good agent will arrange for an escalator clause to be included in your contract, which provides a bonus payment should your book accomplish a specific feat, such as making a bestseller list or being picked up by a book-of-the-month club. Without an agent, you have no leverage to negotiate better terms.

- **An agent acts as a buffer.** The publishing industry is a business. An agent acts as buffer between you and the business issues so you can maintain a creative relationship with your editor and focus on writing.

Agents deal with rejection letters, so you do not have to think about them. Agents track payments and ensure you are paid on schedule. An agent also handles publicity, marketing, and legal aspects of your career and can offer guidance as business issues arise.

- **An agent will ensure you receive better subsidiary rights.** Subsidiary rights are secondary rights that can be sold with a book. They include translation rights, audio rights, film rights, book club rights, serial rights, foreign rights, and additional rights. Agents negotiate to retain some of these rights and take responsibility for selling them on your behalf: responding to inquiries, sending out books, handling paperwork, and arranging deals. Successful agents use co-agents in Hollywood to try to sell the movie and television rights for your book, creating additional revenue and royalties. Without an agent, the publisher will often retain these rights.

- **An agent has contacts to help your career.** An agent's network can help you land endorsements and forewords from other authors and experts, publicity tie-ins, teaching engagements, speaking opportunities, media coverage, and more writing assignments.

- **An agent is your advocate.** Editors may have 30 titles to edit each year and are forced to prioritize them. Titles with agents take priority at publishing houses and receive more attention from editors then books without agent representation. Agents will advocate for quality book cover designs, higher marketing budgets, and better placement. If an editor leaves the company, an agent will work to ensure the new editor assigned to your book is enthusiastic about it being published. Without an agent, if your editor leaves, you and your project will be orphaned. If your first book under-performs and your publisher drops you, your agent has a vested interest in finding another publisher for you. Without an agent, if your first book is not successful, you will have a difficult time finding another agent or publisher for subsequent books. Your agent may be the only stable element of your writing career.

HOW TO KNOW WHEN YOU ARE READY FOR AN AGENT

Now that you understand what a literary agent can do for you and have decided to acquire one, how do you know when you are ready for an agent? Below are questions to consider:

- **Have you explored all options for publishing your book?** Agents only sell to large and mid-size publishers, so your first task is to determine if traditional publishing with a large publishing house is the best option for your book. If you write poetry, short story collections, academic books, or specialized nonfiction, or if your writing focuses on a specific area, such as bed and breakfast inns of Maine, you may fare better approaching small publishers directly. If you wish to retain complete control of your project, then you might choose to self-publish your work and forego hiring an agent to sell your book to a traditional publisher.

- **Have you researched agents and created an agent file?** Individual agents within each literary agency represent specific types of books. If you approach an agent who does not consider your particular genre, you have wasted your time submitting a pitch. A well-researched and focused approach will help you acquire the right agent quickly. *Chapter 3 details how to find and research agents, and Chapter 4 teaches you how to create an effective agent file based on your specific needs.*

- **Do you have a pitch package?** An agent expects you to know the selling points of your book and be able to convey them effectively with your pitch package. For fiction writers, a pitch package consists of a query letter, synopsis, and completed manuscript. For nonfiction writers, your pitch package is made up of a query letter, book proposal, and two sample chapters. *Chapter 4 outlines the essential requirements of a pitch package.*

- **Is your book proposal or manuscript polished?** Fiction and narrative nonfiction writers must have a completed manuscript prior to approaching an agent. It should be professionally edited, proofread, and critiqued to ensure it is the best it can be. Nonfiction writers' book proposals should be polished and provide a complete picture of the finished work. *Chapter 6 shows you how to create the book proposal, and Chapter 8 provides tips for polishing and packaging your manuscript.*

- **Is your novel or book idea marketable?** A key component to acquiring an agent and publishing deal is a marketable product. Below are questions you can answer to determine the marketability of your idea or book to an agent.

  1. *Does a nearly identical book already exist?*
     If a book already exists that is almost identical to your idea you will have trouble selling yours to an agent or publisher. You will need to ensure and show an agent how your book will be better than the ones already on the market.

  2. *How large is the potential audience for your book?* Who will buy your book? If only you and your parents are interested in your book's subject, a publisher or agent will not be begging for your manuscript. A valuable resource for determining how many potential readers there are for your subject matter is to browse the sales ranks of similar books on the market and review the bestseller lists in your genre. *Publishers Weekly* magazine online (**www.publishersweekly.com**) provides bestseller lists, and columns on "Retail Sales" and "Trends and Topics" that you may find helpful. *The New York Times'* book review section (**www.nytimes.com/pages/books**) also lists bestsellers by category. The Web site Titlez (**www.titlez.com**) allows you to track Amazon.com℠ sales rank history by keyword, title, or author and compare similar books by genre or title.

  3. *Does your book have series potential?*
     Spin-off or series potential is not mandatory to sell your manuscript or book idea, but an agent or publisher is more interested in projects that beget more product. Books with spin-off or series potential are considered more valuable.

- **Do you have a platform and strong promotion plan?** Agents and publishers prefer authors who have an established platform. If you are a nonfiction writer, especially, your ability to promote your book will be vital for acquiring an agent and a book deal. *Chapter 3 outlines how to establish and grow your author platform and build credentials.*

- **Have you mapped out a writing career?** Agents represent writing careers, not authors who write only one book. They look for authors who have a vision and plan for their writing careers. Before approaching an agent you should have a clear understanding of what you want to accomplish with your writing and the next step along your path as an author.

Checklist for Fiction Writers

❑ Agent file

❑ Query letter

❑ Synopsis

❑ Completed novel

❑ Polished and critiqued manuscript

❑ Marketable book

❑ Author platform

❑ Career map

Checklist for Nonfiction Writers

❑ Agent file

❑ Query letter

❑ Book proposal

❑ Sample chapters or completed manuscript (narrative nonfiction only)

❑ Marketable idea

❑ Author platform and promotional plan

❑ Career map

CASE STUDY: "HOW I ACQUIRED MY AGENT"

David Meerman Scott
Web site — www.davidmeermanscott.com
Blog — www.webinknow.com
Twitter — http://twiter.com//dmscott

Books: *The New Rules of Marketing and PR: How to Use News Releases, Blogs, Viral Marketing and Online Media to Reach Buyers Directly* (2007, John Wiley & Sons, Inc.), *World Wide Rave: Creating Triggers that Get Millions of People to Spread Your Ideas and Share Your Stories* (2009, John Wiley & Sons, Inc.)

Genre: Nonfiction (business)

Agent: Bill Gladstone, Waterside Productions, Inc.

I wrote a free e-book in January 2006 and released it on my blog. The free e-book became an immediate hit. Dozens of bloggers linked to it within days and it had 50,000 downloads in the first month. I wanted to expand the ideas into a business book and on the recommendation of a friend; I contacted Bill Gladstone at Waterside Productions.

My pitch was very simple, I told Bill that I had 50,000 downloads of my free e-book in a month and that many bloggers were talking up my ideas. He signed me immediately.

We worked on a proposal together and sold the book to John Wiley and Sons, Inc. *The New Rules of Marketing and PR: How to Use News Releases, Blogs, Podcasting, Viral Marketing and Online Media to Reach Buyers Directly* came out in hardcover in June 2007. The paperback edition was released in January 2009 and a second edition is scheduled for March 2010. The book spent months on the *BusinessWeek* bestseller list and is now published in 24 languages.

Since then, I have also published *World Wide Rave: Creating Triggers that Get Millions of People to Spread Your Ideas and Share Your Stories*, also with Wiley and with Bill as the agent.

What I have learned from this experience and through many discussions with other authors and publishers is that in order to get a business book published, you need to prove to agents and publishers that your book will sell. One of the best ways to do that is to show, through your Web content (e-books, blog, YouTube[SM] videos, and so on) that you are popular and will sell books. My recommendation for those who want to publish a business book is to focus attention on building an online platform. Without one, you are unlikely to attract the attention of agents and publishers.

Understanding the Market

To acquire an agent, it is important to know what is happening in the market, where you fit in, and what agents want. The more understanding you have, the better you can position yourself.

WHAT AGENTS LOOK FOR

The overwhelming majority of material agents receive is unpublishable or poorly presented. Literary agents say they accept 1 percent of submissions. They reject the other 99 percent of submissions because:

- The material is poorly written, and/or

- The agent does not think he or she can sell it

Fast Facts	
• 87 percent of content is considered amateurish and unpublishable.	• 3 percent has a potential market, but is poorly written or researched.
• 4 percent is considered quality material, but it lacks a target market.	• 1 percent is considered potentially good material if the writing is revised and polished.
• 4 percent is considered good writing, but the market for it is already saturated.	• 1 percent is considered well written, promising, and ready to be presented to a publisher.

With their understanding of what publishers are looking for, agents consider these factors prior to representing an author's work:

- The quality of your writing

- The marketability of the book

- Potential for subsidiary rights

- Your author platform

- Your potential writing career

The quality of your writing

Agents want original, well-written, and non-derivative works. A writer's understanding of his genre as well as his readers' expectations is essential to produce quality material. *See the "Understanding Your Genre" section for tips.*

For fiction, agents are looking for:

- A powerful, distinctive 'voice'

- Unique storyline

- Original, compelling, well-crafted sentences

- Interesting characters

- Dialogue that reveals character and subtext

- Narrative that evokes images

- An intriguing and immediate opening hook that contains action, conflict, and crisis

For nonfiction, agents look for:

- A strong narrative element

- A structure that flows logically and leads the reader to a specific goal

- Writing that delivers help to solve a problem or make one's life better

The marketability of the book

Agents consider how many readers the book will attract. If you write nonfiction and you can identify a large, specific group of potential readers who want or need what you plan to write about, then you will increase your chances of snagging an agent and a book deal.

For fiction authors, if you write in a genre that sells particularly well, an agent has more opportunity to sell your book. If the market is already saturated — such as young adult novels about teen vampires or nonfiction books on the next best diet — unless you can prove that your manuscript is unique and that you have an established network of readers, your agent will consider it a hard sell and take a pass. Agents may also consider whether a book will tie in with current events that will help sell it to readers.

Potential for subsidiary rights

Subsidiary rights present a potential bounty of revenue for an author, and hence, an author's agent. If your book has the possibility to be serialized, made into a film or television movie, become a book-of-the-month club selection, or merchandised in other ways, an agent will weigh this information when considering you as a client.

Your author platform

Agents expect nonfiction authors to have an established platform before approaching them for representation. In particular, agents say they look for a strong Web presence including a Web site or blog and social media networking, which builds the writer's readership base. If a book is synergistic with an author's brand, an agent sees potential for additional promotion, publicity, and sales. Though a platform is less important for fiction writers, if you are a first-time novelist and can show you have an established platform or credentials, you increase your chances for representation.

Your potential writing career

For a literary agent, investing in a writer requires a commitment of time and resources, and the agent's reputation. The agent wants to ensure his or her commitment is worth the effort by investing in an author who will have a career in writing; an author who will produce more than one book; and one who is passionate about promoting and sustaining his or her writing career.

PUBLISHING TRENDS AND SEASONS

If you attend writer's conferences, read writing magazines, or subscribe to industry newsletters or blogs, you are bound to hear predictions from the 'experts' that *this* type of writing is in and *that* type of book is out. *Chick-lit is dead and memoirs do not sell. No one reads western novels anymore. Gothic romance is the next big thing.* Such pronouncements should not interfere with your primary goal, which is to write an exceptional manuscript or book proposal and acquire an agent to sell your book. Know the market, but do not worry about the market.

Popular trends

Whenever a book becomes a bestseller, publishers and readers look for more of the same. When *Marley and Me* by John Grogan became a hit, publishers released similar books about dogs and their owners, and readers devoured them — for a while. Eventually, the market becomes saturated and readers grow tired of reading the same story or subject matter.

Publishing trends come and go. A popular topic today will be different a year from now. For that reason, it is best to be aware of trends, but do not write to trends. Focus your writing on what you love. You must be invested in and passionate about your subject. Otherwise, you will not be able to convey enthusiasm to an agent, publisher, or reader.

Timeliness and relevance

If your topic is timely and relevant, agents will consider that aspect of your manuscript when considering representing it. Following a current 'popular trend' is not advised, but being aware of lifestyle shifts and readers' needs may benefit your book's potential sales.

Think about ways your book may be tied to current events and book sales. The economic downturn that began in 2007, concern for the environment, depletion of natural resources, and an aging generation of baby-boomers are just four major elements affecting readers' lifestyles.

As baby boomers age, they are planning for their parents' medical and caretaker needs and focusing on staying healthy and in-shape. The financial crisis that began in 2007 has lead many people to look for jobs by using unique methods, repair their credit and create debt strategies, avoid foreclosure, and create new streams of revenue. These trends have lead to an increase in entrepreneurship and a need for books on running and marketing small businesses. Many readers are looking for ways to save money by doing their own repairs and home improvements, which creates a rise in do-it-yourself-book sales; or lowering their budgets by vacationing close to home, leading to an increase in sales of regional and local travel books. Environmental concern has created an enormous opportunity for going green books.

Some books are tied to the calendar. Everything from the twentieth anniversary in 2009 of the Tiananmen Square uprising, to the thirtieth anniversary in 2007 of the release of the film "Star Wars" can create reader interest in a specific subject. In 2009, readers saw the release of a plethora of historical books commemorating the bicentennial of Abraham Lincoln's birth.

Seasonal publishing

Publishers tend to release certain types of books at specific times of the year. Here is a typical breakdown of seasonal publishing:

January

Readers are planning for the year and focusing on their resolutions. Publishers release books on fitness, health, dieting, parenting, weddings, tax preparations, relationships, starting a business, home improvements, daily planners/calendars, budgeting, travel, how-to, and self-help.

February

February produces an increase in romance novels, relationship self-help books, and books celebrating Black History Month.

March, April, and May

Easter, Passover, and Mother's Day books are released and books for dads, graduates, and sports fans are published.

June, July, and August

Summer brings books for beach reading, travel getaways, grilling and barbecuing, and Father's Day.

September and October

Books by bestselling authors are often launched this time of year, along with re-releases of standards and classic that may be required high school or university reading. Halloween books, gothic romance, thrillers, and horror are also popular genres.

November and December

Gift books, holiday books, cookbooks, craft books, books by bestselling authors, and calendars are big-sellers during the holiday season.

UNDERSTANDING YOUR GENRE

Genre is a set of criteria for a category of composition. A book's genre helps inform a potential reader what to expect emotionally, structurally, and intellectually. Genre, then, creates a set of expectations and it is your job as the writer to know what those expectations are and deliver them to the reader. Bookstores categorize books by genre making it easy for readers to find the type of books they enjoy. Understanding your genre also assists you in marketing your manuscript or book idea effectively. *Appendix IV includes definitions for all listed genres and subgenres.*

It is important to categorize your genre accurately. If you label your novel as romance but it is actually a thriller that includes a romance, you risk the chance of losing a potential agent because you pitched it incorrectly.

Literary fiction

The writing style or voice of the author, the in-depth exploration of characters, and the profound use of symbolism, imagery, and theme is what distinguishes literary fiction from mainstream or genre fiction. Literary fiction may fall into any of the categories of the fiction genre, but appeals to a smaller audience than genre fiction. It is considered to be of greater artistic and cultural value. Examples of literary fiction are *Cold Mountain* by Charles Frazier, *To Kill A Mockingbird* by Harper Lee, and Ian McEwan's *Atonement*.

Genre fiction

Genre fiction, also called popular fiction, mainstream fiction, or commercial fiction, is plot-driven and attracts a wider audience than literary fiction. Each category and sub-genre has specific conventions and formulas to meet readers' expectations. You will find many of the subcategories overlap.

Romance

According to the Romance Writers of America, the main plot of a romance novel must center on the hero and the heroine as they develop romantic love for each other. Romance novels provide an emotionally satisfying and optimistic ending.

Popular authors and books include: *Wish for Love* by Barbara Cartland, *Mistress of Mellyn* by Victoria Holt, and *Matters of the Heart* by Danielle Steel.

Sub-genres include: Chick-Lit, Christian, Contemporary, Fantasy, Erotica, Glitz/ Glamour, Historical, Multicultural, Paranormal, Romantic Comedy, Romantic Suspense, Sensual, Spicy, Sweet, and Young Adult.

Horror

According to the Horror Writers Association, horror novels are primarily about emotion. It is writing that delves deep inside and forces readers to confront who they are, to examine what they are afraid of, and to wonder what lies ahead down the road of life.

Popular authors and books include: *Carrie* by Stephen King, *Mister B. Gone* by Clive Barker, *Relentless* by Dean Koontz, *Interview with the Vampire* by Anne Rice, and *The Pit and the Pendulum* by Edgar Allan Poe.

Sub-genres include: Child in Peril, Comic Horror, Creepy Kids, Dark Fantasy, Dark Mystery / Noir, Erotic Vampire, Fabulist, Gothic, Hauntings, Historical, Magical Realism, Psychological, Quiet Horror, Religious, Science-Fiction Horror, Splatter / Splatterpunk, Supernatural Menace, Technology, Weird Tales, Young Adult, and Zombie.

Thriller/Suspense

According to the International Thriller Writers Association, Inc., thriller stories center on a complex plot and present ordinary people caught in extraordinary circumstances; they are typified by the protagonist running for his or her life, before turning to face and ultimately triumph over the danger.

Popular authors and books include: *Scarpeta* by Patricia Cornwell, *Presumed Innocent* by Scott Turow, *The Client* by John Grisham, *Clear and Present Danger* by Tom Clancy, *Kiss The Girls* by James Patterson, and *Deep Black Conspiracy* by Stephen Coonts.

Sub-genres include: Action, Comic, Conspiracy, Crime, Disaster, Eco-Thriller, Erotic, Espionage, Forensic, Historical, Horror, Legal, Medical, Military, Police Procedural, Political Intrigue, Psychological, Romantic, Supernatural, and Technological.

Science Fiction/Fantasy

Science fiction novels center on the imagined impact of science on society, while fantasy novels include fantastic elements, such as magic and supernatural forms, inspired from mythology and folklore to convey the story, plot, and theme.

Popular authors and books include: *Lord of the Rings* by J.R.R. Tolkein, *I, Robot* by Isaac Asimov, *Fahrenheit 451* by Ray Bradbury, *War of the Worlds* by H.G. Wells, and *2001: A Space Odyssey* by Arthur Clarke.

Sub-genres include: Arthurian Fantasy, Bangsian Fantasy, Biopunk, Children's Fantasy, Comic, Cyberpunk, Dark Fantasy, Dystopian, Erotic, Game-Related Fantasy, Hard Science Fiction, Heroic Fantasy, High/Epic Fantasy, Historical, Mundane Science Fiction, Military Science Fiction, Mystery Science Fiction, Mythic Fiction, New Age, Post-Apocalyptic, Romance, Religious, Science Fantasy, Social Science Fiction, Soft Science Fiction, Space Opera, Spy-Fi, Steampunk, Superheroes, Sword and Sorcery, Thriller Science Fiction, Time-Travel, Urban Fantasy, Vampire, Wuxia, and Young Adult.

Mystery/Crime

Mystery novels revolve around a crime that needs to be solved. Characteristics of crime fiction include intrigue, victims, clues, suspects, and an investigation.

Popular authors and books include: *L.A. Confidential* by James Ellroy, *Scat* by Carl Hiaasen, *The Maltese Falcon* by Dashiell Hammett, *Swan Peak* by James Lee Burke, *Blood Work* by Michael Connelly, and *The Big Sleep* by Raymond Chandler.

Sub-genres include: Amateur Detective, Child in Peril, Classic Whodunit, Comic (Bumbling Detective), Cozy, Courtroom Drama, Dark Thriller, Espionage, Forensic, Heists and Capers, Historical, Inverted, Locked Room, Medical, Police Procedural, Private Detective, Psychological Suspense, Romantic, Technothriller, Thriller, Woman in Jeopardy, and Young Adult.

Westerns

Western novels, also referred to as "novels of the west," often convey themes of honor, inequality, and sacrifice, and are set primarily in the western part of the United States, Mexico, South America, Western Canada, and Australia. Though most Westerns are set during the late 1800s, modern writers are not restricted to a specific time period.

Popular authors and books include: *Riders of the Purple Sage* by Zane Grey, *Under the Sweetwater Rim* by Louis L'Amour, *Open Range* by Lauran Paine, *Appaloosa* by Robert B. Parker, and *3:10 to Yuma* by Elmore Leonard.

Sub-genres include: Frontier and Pioneer.

Religious/Inspirational

Religious or inspirational novels deal with religious themes (for example Christian themes, such as God, sin, salvation, sacrifice, redemption, and service to others) and incorporate a religious worldview.

Popular authors and books include: *The Shack* by William P. Young, *A Christmas to Die For* by Marta Perry, and *The Reckoning* by Beverly Lewis.

Sub-genres include: Biblical, Christian, Historical, Mystery, Romance, Science Fiction / Fantasy, and Visionary.

Action–Adventure

Action-Adventure novels are characterized by gritty, fast-paced, physical, and violent action with an emphasis on danger. They are set in exotic locales and offer little character development.

Popular authors and books include: *Corsair* by Clive Cussler, *Live or Let Die* by Ian Fleming, and *Designated Targets* by John Birmingham.

Sub-genres include: Disaster Adventure, Espionage Adventure, Industrial/Financial, Medical, Male-Action Adventure, Political Intrigue, Military and Naval, Soft Adventure, Survival Adventure, Thriller Adventure, and Western Adventure.

Historical

Historical novels dramatize past events and characters; they present believable and plausible representations of history.

Popular authors and books include: *The White Queen* by Phillipa Gregory, *Centennial* by James Michener, *The Knight* and the *Rose* by Barbara Erksine, and *The Archer's Tale* by Bernard Cornwell.

Sub-genres include: Alternate Histories, Pseudo-Histories, Time-Slip novels, Historical Fantasies, and Multiple-Time novels.

Young Adult

Young adult novels are written specifically for adolescents, ages 12 to 18. The protagonist of the story is a young adult and the plot revolves around his or her point of view. YA stories span the entire spectrum of fiction genres and focus on the challenges of adolescence and coming of age.

Popular authors and books include: *Harry Potter and the Sorcerer's Stone* by J.K. Rowling, the *Twilight* series by Stephanie Meyer, and *Forever* by Judy Blume.

Women's Fiction

Women's fiction focuses on women's issues and their relationships with their families and friends. They revolve around a theme of female empowerment. These novels include strong female protagonists and portray women triumphing over adversity. These stories conclude with a life-affirming message. Both male and female writers author women's fiction.

Popular authors and books include:, *I'll Take Manhattan* by Judith Krantz, *After This* by Alice McDermott, *Back When We Were Grownups* by Anne Tyler, *My Sister's Keeper* by Jodi Picoult, and *Sex and the City* by Candace Bushnell.

Sub-genres include: Chick-Lit, Domestic Dramas, Erotic Thrillers, Family Sagas, Historical Romances, Kitchen Fiction, Lipstick Fiction, Mom Novel, and Single Women.

Fiction Genre	Average Word Count
Action-Adventure	75,000 to 85,000
Historical	85,000 to 110,000
Horror	75,000 to 85,000

Literary Fiction	85,000 to 110,000
Mystery / Crime	75,000 to 90,000
Religious / Inspirational	80,000 to 90,000
Romance	75,000 to 100,000
Science Fiction / Fantasy	80,000 to 115,000
Thriller / Suspense	85,000 to 100,000
Western	55,000 to 80,000
Women's Fiction	80,000 to 100,000
Young Adult	50,000 to 75,000

Nonfiction

Nonfiction books stand or fall on the delivery of the promise to help the reader. Regardless of your genre, as a nonfiction writer, you either:

- **Help the reader fix a problem.** Self-help, how-to, reference, inspirational, travel guides, and cookbooks usually serve this purpose.

- **Provide information to expand a reader's knowledge and worldview.** This is the intent of most narrative nonfiction works and includes memoirs, biographies, autobiographies, historical accounts, and books on current events.

The most effective way to understand the nonfiction genre is to peruse complementary, as well as competitive, books in the same genre as your book idea. Analyze the books in your niche and note:

- The layout — Do most contain sidebars, case studies, anecdotes, photos, or charts?

- The structure — The number of chapters and sections, and the overall book length.

- The delivery — Is the style casual or formal: Is the tone fun and motivational, or sincere and cautionary?

- The content — Is the manuscript packed with hard-hitting information, statistical/technical overload, complex theories, or detailed historical accounts? Or, does it contain simple step-by-step instructions, homespun advice, basic processes, or easily understood philosophy?

- The purpose — Is it to educate, motivate, expose, entertain, convince, inspire, or connect and share the human experience?

How-to

How-to books outsell every other nonfiction genre. Within the how-to niche, the best-selling categories are: Business/Leadership/Career, Parenting, Sex, Money/Finances, Dieting/Weight Loss, and Health/Fitness. How-to books are filled with instructions, valuable information, tips, suggestions, examples, and illustrations. Information is presented sequentially with each chapter supporting the overall concept. These books conclude with the reader achieving a specific "goal."

Books: *Starting on a Shoestring: Building a Business without a Bankroll* by Arnold S. Goldstein, *Scrapbook Basics* by Michele Gebrandt, and *WordPress for Dummies* by Lisa Sabin-Wilson.

Self-help

Self-Help books encompass the realm of psychology. The most popular category is Relationships. Self-help books have more examples than how-to books. The author's style is casual, as if conversing with an old friend across the table.

Books: *Surviving the Breakup* by Judith S. Wallerstein and Joan B. Kelly, *From Panic to Power* by Lucinda Bassett, and *Overcoming Depression* by Demetri Papolos.

Travel guides

Travel guidebooks are always in demand, especially if they cover a location that has not been saturated or take a fresh spin on a topic, such as the top 100 romantic places to kiss. Travel guides require detailed research and must provide all the necessary information and tips to help the reader successfully plan a trip to the destination.

Books: *Away for the Weekend* by Eleanor Berman, and *Europe on $5 a Day* by Arthur Frommer.

Cooking and food

Hundreds of new cookbooks are published each year. To succeed in this competitive genre you need a distinctive theme that captures the reader's attention. Cookbooks incorporate vibrant photos, systematic detailed instructions, and a casual, 'you-can-do-it,' style.

Books: *Almost Vegetarian* by Diana Shaw, *The Complete Book of Bread Machine Baking* by Kristi Fuller, and *The Santa Monica Farmer's Market Cookbook* by Amelia Saltsman.

Inspirational/religious/spiritual/metaphysical

Religious, inspirational, and spiritual books share themes of a particular belief system and provide wisdom, motivation, and advice to guide readers to live a full life in harmony with specific concepts. Metaphysical books investigate principles of reality that transcend science, such as astrology, numerology, and psychic ability. These books uplift readers' spirits and require an author who is closely attuned to the readership: who the readers are, what they assume, and their "language." The writer must have a full understanding of the history of the subject.

Books: *The Purpose-Driven Life* by Rick Warren, *Conversations with God* by Neale Donald Walsch, and *The Case for Faith* by Lee Strobel.

Reference

A reference book contains authoritative facts. Successful reference books never go out-of-date. Authors can simply update the content every five to eight years. Popular reference categories include Computer and Internet books as well as Directories. "Coffee table" books also fall under this genre and Architecture, Art, and Photography are popular subgenres.

Books: *The Quotable Star Wars* by Stephen J. Sansweet, *The Big Book of 60,000 Baby Names* by Diane Stafford, and *The 21st Century Crossword Puzzle Dictionary* by Kevin McCann and Mark Diehl.

Humor

Humor books are filled with content that is witty and entertaining. They are usually given as gifts. They are short, funny, and have an identifiable audience, such as cat owners, golfers, or parents.

Books: *If Dogs Could Talk* by Joel Zadak, *The Women's Daily Irony Supplement* by Judy Gruen, and *Unusually Stupid Americans* by Ross and Kathryn Petras.

Medical and science

Medical and science books enlighten and educate readers about the medical and scientific fields. They can be successful sellers. They require extensive research, interviewing, and fact checking. They incorporate charts, graphs, illustrations, and a thorough glossary.

Books: *A Brief History of Time* by Stephen Hawking, and *The Physics of Star Trek* by Lawrence M. Krauss.

Narrative nonfiction

Narrative nonfiction, also referred to as creative nonfiction, is truthful writing that reads like a novel. It straddles the line between nonfiction and fiction, incorporating storytelling techniques such as plot, conflict, and dialogue. Narrative nonfiction requires:

- Factual subject matter

- Exhaustive research

- Compelling narrative or a literary prose style

History

History books have a scholarly tone and are often written by experts — not necessarily a professional historian, but at least someone who has extensively studied the subject. Historical stories are compelling to readers when they evoke a sense of place by maintaining the customs, culture, and knowledge of the period, as well as providing relevance to our lives today, or revealing something new about a well-known, or little-known, event. Military books are considered a sub-genre of history.

Popular books and authors: *Killing Pablo* and *Black Hawk Down* by Mark Bowden, *Band of Brothers* by Stephen E. Ambrose, *1776* by David McCullough, *How The Irish Saved Civilization* by Thomas Cahill, and *Seabiscuit* by Laura Hillenbrand.

Adventure

Adventure books consist of a man-against-nature story. They have an extreme and dramatic quality and are set in an exotic location.

Popular books and authors: *Into the Wild* and *Into Thin Air* by Jon Krakauer, and *The Perfect Storm* by Sebastian Junger.

Travelogues

Travelogues incorporate the author's travel experience and may include travel guide details about the destination.

Popular books and authors: *A Walk in the Woods* and *In a Sunburned Country* by Bill Bryson, and *Under The Tuscan Sun* by Frances Mayes.

Biography

Along with extensive research and minute fact verification, biographies require the author to be devoted to the subject matter, but objective enough to go wherever the truth may lead in order to create an accurate portrayal. Biographies come with their own set of challenges, such as:

- Will the subject (if alive) or the family cooperate with the telling of his or her story?

- How will 'fans' of the subject respond to negative revelations?

- Has the subject been covered thoroughly or do you have a new perspective or theory to present to readers?

- Does the subject warrant cradle-to-grave coverage or is there one inspirational event or portion of your subject's life worthy of exploration?

Popular books and authors: *John Adams* by David McCullough, *JFK* by James W. Douglass, and *The Snowball: Warren Buffett and the Business of Life* by Alice Schroeder.

Memoir

The challenge of memoir is to write a personal account, whether tragic or inspiring, that has a universal connection. Memoirs must transcend the personal and become a shared experience for readers.

Popular books and authors: *Angela's Ashes* by Frank McCourt, *Running with Scissors* by Augusten Burroughs, and *Dreams of My Father* by Barack Obama.

True crime

True Crime accounts incorporate the art of the newspaper reporter. It requires investigative, analytical attention to detail, and some understanding of police and forensic procedures. The author must present an in-depth study of the cast of characters, the victim's family, the detectives, the lawyers, and the perpetrator, and effectively capture and convey what is identifiable and intriguing.

Popular books and authors: *In Cold Blood* by Truman Capote, *And The Sea Will Tell* by Vincent Bugliosi, *The Stranger Beside Me* by Ann Rule, *The Devil In The White City* by Erik Larson, *Echoes in the Darkness* by Joseph Wambaugh, and *The Executioner's Song* by Norman Mailer.

CASE STUDY: "HOW I ACQUIRED MY AGENT"

Greg Gutierrez
Telephone — 619.405.9496
Web site — www.greggutierrez.com

Books: *Zen and the Art of Surfing*

Genre: A cross between mainstream fiction and literary fiction

Agent: Victoria Sanders of Victoria Sanders and Associates, LLC

When I finished my novel, I decided I wanted to find a commercial publisher. I queried about 50 agents with no luck prior to pitching Victoria Sanders.

What I learned from the rejections is that I needed to cut the manuscript to fewer than 100,000 words, and ensure my writing was void of any clichés and was "showing, not telling." I learned not to get bitter, but to get better.

I approached Victoria because I loved the other authors she represents. The opening line of my query letter, "What happens when a lost man finds Christ, only to lose his soul?" is what grabbed her attention. She requested to read my complete manuscript within two weeks of my pitch and offered to represent me. Her agency fell in love with my work and I knew she was the right fit. My author platform was also a key selling point (I write stories for surfing magazines and had my collection, *Zen and the Art of Surfing*, published through a grant.)

Victoria made some requests for changes and we edited and added a key passage over the course of four months. I was and am still wide open to follow my agent's direction — she is the professional. We have not sold the manuscript to a publisher yet, but I would do whatever is necessary to help my agent sell it. If she asked me to I would fly to New York in a moment. I have spent this time writing my next novel, The Evening Doorman.

My advice to have a smooth and successful relationship with your agent is to choose an agent you believe in, and who believes in you. And then, follow her lead.

Establishing Your Author Platform and Building Credentials

A platform is an author's media exposure and abilities to develop a potential group of readers. If you are a nonfiction writer, you must have an established platform. Without one, you will not land a book deal, and you will not acquire an agent. There are no exceptions to this publishing industry rule. No matter how outstanding the content may be, an author platform is essential to sell your book. A publisher will not commit to signing an author and releasing a book unless they know the writer has a large following of potential readers.

A writer seeking an agent for commercial publication cannot ignore this fact. The reality of this requirement is even highlighted at publishing industry events such as the annual Writer's Digest Conference, "The Business of Getting Published," which emphasizes seminars on the topic of platform building, networking, and social media.

If you are a fiction writer or author of narrative nonfiction, having a platform is helpful, though not absolutely necessary. With fiction and narrative nonfiction, agents and publishers consider the author's credentials. However, in the competitive literary world, anything you can do to show an agent and an editor you have a built-in readership will increase your chances of seeing your book in print.

ESTABLISHING A PLATFORM

A platform encompasses the ways you are visible and attracting potential readers. It conveys your expertise and influence. If you are recognized as a leader on a specific topic, then you have attained a successful platform. Building a platform requires substantial effort and time. It takes about three years to build reputation, credibility, and an extensive following. At the minimum, you will need to invest a year in developing your platform before pitching a nonfiction book idea to an agent.

Platforms that impress agents and publishers:

- Speaking in front of 50,000 people per year (either all at one time or divided into several speaking engagements).

- Repeat expert guest segments on national television.

- A blog, mailing list, or subscriber list of at least 50,000 potential readers.

- A video on YouTube^{SM} that has received more than one million hits.

- Weekly guest appearances on a national radio show or hosting your own national radio show.

- A daily or weekly column in a national, syndicated newspaper or a monthly column in a magazine with wide circulation.

Strategies for both nonfiction and fiction writers to build a platform:

Develop and promote your expertise

Expertise includes your knowledge on a particular topic and how well others regard you. You must earn the respect and trust of others to be considered a credible expert. This is developed through earning degrees, experience in the field, testimonials, endorsements, speaking engagements, and teaching your skills to others.

Fiction writers can also become established as experts in particular niches, such as:

- A time period
- A specific theme, such as individuality or redemption
- A topic, for instance legal corruption or criminal forensics
- A location, for example New England or the southwest

Jodi Picoult effectively asserts her niche in her Web site's tagline "Novels About Family, Relationships, and Love." Phillipa Gregory writes books centered on English nobility in the 15th, 16th, and 17th centuries and is known as "the queen of royal" novels. John Grisham uses his expertise as a lawyer and politician to construct legal thrillers, and Stephen King sets most of his novels in Maine.

Create a Web site

Every potential author needs a Web site. This is your home base on the Internet where you can place excerpts from your forthcoming book, photo headshots, contact information, videos, and links to your Facebook[SM] and Twitter[SM] profiles. If you already have a Web site when you begin approaching media, you will have an edge over other writers.

Brand yourself

Establish an author identity and use it consistently throughout your material. Your personal brand is how you package and present yourself to readers to distinguish and differentiate yourself from other writers.

Set up a blog

The wider your Web presence the better. A blog adds to your credibility, helps you establish your expertise, and provides a means to capture potential readers for your database. Make a writing plan and consistently post to your blog. If you are a nonfiction writer, you should write about your expertise on your niche topic. Fiction writers can blog about their genre or experiences, post short stories, interview other writers, or do book reviews. Comment on other author's blogs and write guest posts to continue to increase traffic to your site.

Create a video

Posting a video on your Web site or blog substantially increases traffic. It also shows potential media outlets how you will perform on television and radio. Be sure to post your video on YouTube℠ (**www.youtube.com**) as well. Visitors to YouTube℠ search for videos the way users of search engines seek keywords. You can shoot a video related to your niche, a trailer for your book, or a captivating scene from your novel that creates interest and curiosity in your story.

Social networking

Social networking is a powerful marketing tool. Facebook℠ (**www.facebook. com**), Twitter℠ (**http://twitter.com**), LinkedIn℠ (**www.linkedin.com**), Red-Room (**www.redroom.com**), and other online networking sites give you access to connections and a platform to share your writing and expertise.

Gather endorsements

Recommendations from successful authors and well-known industry leaders are a potent sales tool. Ask your connections if they can provide testimonials or endorsements of your work or writing.

Podcasts

Hosting a weekly syndicated audio recording or podcast can introduce you to a wide audience of followers. The segments can also be presented to radio programmers to show your potential as a guest on one of their shows. Podcasts can be created around a serialized version of your forthcoming book, interviews with writers in the same genre, or based on topics within your specialized niche of expertise. Podcasts can be created using free software available from Audacity™ (**http://audacity.sourceforge.net**) and syndicated through iTunes℠ (**www.itunes.com**).

Newsletters

Your Web site and blog should include an opt-in page to capture subscribers and potential readers of your upcoming book. Stay in contact with your subscribers with a weekly or monthly e-zine or newsletter that provides valuable content they have shown an interest in reading. Services such as ConstantContact℠ (**www.constantcontact.com**) and VerticalResponse℠ (**www.verticalresponse. com**) make it easy and affordable to create a customized newsletter, e-mail it to your subscribers, and manage your subscriptions.

Offer excerpts

Posting excerpts from your manuscript on your Web site or blog encourages reader interest and establishes trust and loyalty. Consider giving away an e-book or mini-book of writings to entice visitors to sign-up and be added to your database.

Additional strategies for nonfiction writers to build a platform:

Create a media kit

Make it easy for journalists and TV reporters to use you as a source for interviews by putting an online media kit on your Web site. Your media kit can include photos/headshots, a list of topics you speak on, sample interview questions, a portfolio of media clips, a backgrounder or bio, excerpts from you book, a calendar of upcoming events or speaking engagements, and press releases.

Write articles

Approach magazines and news outlets that would be receptive to an article, op-ed, or column on your niche topic. Write articles on your area of expertise and distribute them on article syndication sites such as EzineArticles (**www.ezinearticles.com**) and document sharing sites including Scribd℠ (**www.scribd.com**). Be sure to include a link to your Web site, blog, and other media outlets in the signature.

Distribute a news release

An online news release has the potential to garner a wide range of media opportunities. A news release is similar to a press release. It is a one-page presentation of newsworthy information of interest to reporters and news agencies. Find a way to tie your expertise to a current event. If your niche is social media marketing and a new study is about to be published that indicates the majority of corporate America now utilizes social media to market their products and services, write a news release stating that information, and align it to your expertise. Conclude with a brief synopsis of your background and include contact information and a link to your online media page.

You can use a news distribution service to disseminate your release. Major U.S. news distribution services include: Business Wire℠ (**www.businesswire.com**), PR Newswire℠ (**www.prnewswire.com**), and PRWeb℠ (**www.prweb.com**). Their services range in price from $200 to $800.

Teach

Turn your topic into a class, workshop, or seminar to attract an audience interested in your subject. Teaching also shows agents and editors your ability to effectively convey ideas. Consider approaching conferences, associations, universities, community colleges, lifelong learning programs, community organizations, or adult education centers to begin teaching. Then transfer your in-person teaching success to online classes and reach an even broader range of potential customers.

Speaking engagements

Opportunities to speak are abundant. Depending on your area of expertise, you may consider approaching businesses, events, conferences, or your local chamber of commerce. If you can line up a network of large venues for speaking engagements it will strongly support your author platform when searching for an agent and publisher. Consider hiring a speaking agent to book bigger engagements.

Radio and television

Send your media kit to local radio and television stations that would be a good fit for your topic. Once you have garnered a few local programs, expand your reach to regional and national platforms.

Magazines and newspapers

Present yourself as a potential expert source to magazine writers and columnists.

BUILDING CREDENTIALS

Credentials differ from a platform. Credentials are your resume or portfolio of work, knowledge, and accomplishments. Credentials are more important for fiction and narrative nonfiction writers.

Five tips for building your resume and portfolio:

1. **Garner publication credits.**
   Have your writing published in four or five well-respected magazines or journals; this provides credibility. Consider pitching a collection of short stories or a serialization of your novel or narrative nonfiction.

2. ***Apply for awards and grants.***

    Winning a prestigious award or grant is a noteworthy addition to your portfolio. You can find a list of available grants and awards published in each issue of *Poets & Writers* magazine.

3. ***Enroll in writing courses or an MFA program.***

    Studying with an acclaimed author or attending an MFA program is an excellent addition to your resume and can lead to valuable connections. *Poets & Writers* magazine offers a "Guide to MFA Programs," which is available on their Web site at **www.pw.org**.

4. ***Apply to writer's residencies.***

    Writer's residencies (also referred to as writer's colonies) are exceptional opportunities to meet and build relationships with established writers as well as add another credential to your portfolio, and many offer free fellowships. Each issue of *Poet & Writers* magazine provides a list of writer's residencies along with detailed application information.

5. ***Pursue an advanced degree.***

    If you write serious narrative nonfiction, such as historical, an agent and publisher may expect you to have a Ph.D. or professorship.

CASE STUDY: "HOW I ACQUIRED MY AGENT"

Jess Haines
Web site — www.jesshaines.com
E-mail — info@jesshaines.com

Books: *Hunted by the Others* (Kensington Publishing Corp., April/May 2010) and two contracted sequels

Genre: Urban fantasy

Agent: Ellen Pepus, Signature Literary Agency

I decided I wanted to acquire an agent mostly as a matter of convenience. I want to focus on my writing, not the business end of making deals or negotiating contracts. I also wanted someone who would be able to guide me through the process and answer my questions about the industry. About five agents rejected me before obtaining my agent. I learned that I needed to do my research before contacting an agent, and narrow down my search to agents who represent my genre.

I was reading Chuck Sambuchino's *Writer's Digest* article, "28 Agents Who Want Your Work" and came across a listing for Ellen Pepus. I did some additional research and checked out her Web site and she looked to be the closest "fit" for my work. Nathan Bransford of Curtis Brown, LTD has a sample query letter format and examples of proper queries on his Web site, so I used those as my guide.

Two weeks after sending my query, Ellen requested to read a few sample chapters and six weeks after that she asked for the full manuscript. I had worked with a critique group, which was extremely helpful, and this led to me revising and polishing it until it was a strong, clean story I felt confident sending out. A month later, she offered to represent me.

I realized she was the right fit as soon as I spoke with her on the phone. I knew she would be a true proponent of my work. She told me what she liked, what she needed from me, and showed genuine interest in my work — as well as being clear on what I needed to do to make my story saleable. Ellen worked with me on edits for about a month, prior to submitting my work to my publisher. Within three months she closed a three-book deal with Kensington Publishing Corp.

My tips for maintaining a good working relationship with an agent are:

- Be patient. You will be doing a lot of waiting every step of the way.

- Treat them the way you want to be treated. Be polite and professional.

- Do not be afraid to ask questions. If you do not know what you are doing, say so. If you are not sure what something means, ask. If you think something is wrong, do not sit on it.

Overall, I learned a lot through the entire process. First, money is supposed to flow to the author. If an "agent" asks you to pay him or anyone else for anything — such as editing, postage, or copy costs — before selling your work, this is a red flag. Second, the work does not end when you find representation — or even after you get a publisher to take on your work. Continue to educate yourself. Stay on top of the industry with resources such as newsletters, agent and editor blogs, and writer forums. That will help you in innumerable ways, from understanding your contract to learning how to market yourself.

Finding and
Selecting an Agent

F inding and selecting an agent who is the right fit for you and your book is essential for the long-term success of your writing career. It involves extensive research and careful consideration.

HOW TO FIND AGENTS

There are many avenues available to find a literary agent. Most authors utilize several resources to locate potential agents.

Referrals

Referrals are the best avenue for finding and contacting an agent. Agents respect and value referrals from an editor, author-client, bookseller, writing expert, or another agent. Ask your associates, friends, and network if they can refer you to an agent.

Conferences and literary events

Conferences, seminars, retreats, book festivals, and workshops provide an opportunity to meet an agent in person. Agents expect writers to approach them at these events. Some conferences even schedule sessions for authors to pitch to agents. The goal is to connect with agents and leave them with a positive impression of you and your work for when you submit your pitch package in the future. Some agents may even ask you to send them your book proposal or manuscript.

Introducing yourself to agents who are a good fit for your writing increases your chances of acquiring an agent and lays the foundation for a future relationship. The benefits of meeting a literary agent in person are: You create enthusiasm for your project before the agent has even read it; the agent gets an idea of your potential promotion by the way you present yourself and your work; and when you submit your query, it will stand out among the masses of letters they receive daily. Most important, nothing replaces a one-on-one connection and the chemistry it can generate.

Attending conferences and other literary events is a strategy that produces results. A *list of national conferences and additional information about each event can be found in Appendix III.*

You can follow the following steps to make the most of your experience:

1. Review the conference Web site to determine the agents who will be attending or speaking and create a list of the agents you wish to approach.

2. Create a plan of how you will spend your time at the event. Prioritize what you know you *must* do and what you would like to do *if time permits.*

3. Complete your pitch package prior to attending the convention so you will be able to send the material immediately upon returning home from the event.

4. When you arrive at the conference, study the map and the program to better navigate the terrain.

5. Plan to attend both educational and social events, and walk the exhibition floor if one is presented. Collect business cards from everyone you meet.

6. Determine the best time to approach your pre-selected agents — this may be early morning, after a round-table or seminar presentation, or at an opening night cocktail reception.

7. Prepare and practice a pitch speech. Create different versions of your pitch: a 15-second pitch, a one-minute pitch, a two-minute pitch, and a three-minute pitch. Remember, an agent's time is valuable. Keep your speech simple, exciting, and compelling. Leave the agent with a desire to know more about your project or story. Pitch the story or idea first and then follow with your credentials, accomplishments, and platform if time allows.

8. Be prepared to answer follow-up questions.

9. Do not ask an agent to read your work or tell him that you will be sending it to his office tomorrow. Wait for an agent to invite you to send your work.

10. As soon as you return home from the conference, send your query letters to the agents who expressed interest. Be sure to mention in the letter that you met them at the conference. Do not send your manuscript, sample chapters, or book proposal unless invited to do so.

Directories

Each year, several literary agent directories are published. Each guide provides detailed information on individual agents, which include the literary agency where the agent works, his contact information, the types of writing he represents, and his submission guidelines. Additional information may also be included such as recent sales, number of annual sales, professional memberships, and total years in business.

Guide to literary agents

The Guide to Literary Agents is published by Writer's Digest Books and contains a listing of more than 800 literary and script agents. The book provides an index of agents categorized by the genre they represent, which allows you to quickly and conveniently find the agents who represent the type of books you write.

Jeff Herman's Guide to Book Publishers, Editors, & Literary Agents

This directory lists 200 agents who are members of Association of Author's Representatives (AAR), and offers additional details that provide a glimpse of the agents' personalities.

Literary Market Place

Literary Market Place is the most comprehensive directory available. Weighing close to 10 pounds, it has more than 2,000 pages of listings along with a hefty price tag — more than $300. If you have access to a large public library, consider perusing this mammoth guide for free.

The Internet

The array and magnitude of information available via the Internet makes it easier than ever to find literary agents for your book. Forums, blogs, online magazines, directories, and search engines offer an abundance of resources.

Publishers Lunch (www.publisherslunch.com)

Publishers Lunch offers a free daily and weekly newsletter that reports on the latest publishing deals and news, including information on the agents involved with the deals and descriptions of the books that sold.

Publishers Marketplace (www.publishersmarketplace.com)

This Web site offers news about the publishing industry as well as a "Search Members" link to obtain contact information for individual agents and literary agencies, and a listing of the Top 10 Most Visited Agents. The site also offers a paid membership service. For a fee of $20 per month you receive:

- Access to the "Top Dealmakers" section where you can search by agent, agency, or genre and obtain information about recent deals with the specifics of the books and the authors.

- A searchable "Who Represents" section.

- Links to current industry news from the "Automat" section, which also includes the tab "Agencies, Agents, Author Advice," a listing of agent and author blogs.

Publishers Weekly (www.publishersweekly.com)

Publishers Weekly online edition provides articles about the book industry, includes a "Search" box to obtain information on literary agents and agencies, and presents a weekly "Deals" column with details about major book deals. They also offer *PW Daily*, a free weekly newsletter delivered to your e-mail inbox. You can subscribe to the virtual edition of *Publishers Weekly* magazine for $180 per year to obtain access to more articles, news, and deal listings.

Writer's Market (www.writersmarket.com)

Writer's Market offers a free newsletter that may yield information about literary agents. You can sign up for it on their Web site. The site also offers a paid service. For $6 per month you receive online access to the database of agents.

Writer's Digest (www.writersdigest.com)

Writer's Digest's Web site is filled with free articles and interviews. They also offer an annual list of the 101 best Web sites for writers (**www.writersdigest. com/101bestsites**) and a free e-mail newsletter.

"Guide to Literary Agents" blog (www.guidetoliteraryagents.com/blog)

"Guide to Literary Agents" is an invaluable blog that offers insight into landing an agent. Each week they post an analysis of a pitch in the "Successful Queries" series, interview an agent in the "Agent Advice" column, and publish articles from authors who obtained agents.

Agency Web sites

You can easily find the URL for a literary agency by using a search engine and inserting the name of the agency. Agency Web sites include a list of clients, recent deals, submission guidelines, and contact information.

Agent Query (www.agentquery.com)

This service provides a free, searchable database of agents and agency information.

QueryTracker (www.querytracker.net)

QueryTracker offers a free list of agents, but the exceptional value of this Web site is found in the research they amass and make available. QueryTracker gathers information that is input into the database by authors submitting queries to agents. This information includes the name of the agent who is pitched, the word count of the manuscript, the genre of the book, the date of the response, the type of response, and the final outcome. The collected data reveals important information about specific agents: The overall number of queries sent to each agent and their accept/reject rates; the genre-specific accept/reject history of an agent; an agent's preferred manuscript word count; and an agent's average response time. For $20 per year, the Web site also offers even more details about specific agents.

Agent Research (www.agentresearch.com)

This Web site offers services ranging in price from free to $360 for access to extensive database with in-depth information about agents.

Writer's community sites and forums

These Web sites offer industry information, forum Q&As, and the opportunity to connect with other writers: Red Room, a social media site for writers (**www.redroom.com**); Absolute Write, an online magazine for beginning and professional writers (**www.absolutewrite.com**); AuthorLink, a source on the publishing world (**www.authorlink.com**); Writing Room, several resources on the art of writing (**www.writingroom.com**); AuthorNation an online community for authors (**www.authornation.com**); and Writing Forums, for creative writing (**www.writingforums.org**).

Agents' blogs

Agents have their own blogs where they write posts about the publishing industry, their expectations, what they are looking for, their clients' book releases, recent sales, and how to submit a pitch. You can use the Google™ blog search function to find a listing of literary agent blogs (**http://blogsearch.google.com**).

Popular agent blogs include:

Nathan Bransford (**http://blog.nathanbransford.com**)
Rachelle Gardner (**http://cba-ramblings.blogspot.com**)
Kristin Nelson (**http://pubrants.blogspot.com**)

Janet Reid (**http://jetreidliterary.blogspot.com**)

Jessica Faust (**http://bookendslitagency.blogspot.com**)

Sarah Crowe (**http://acrowesnest.blogspot.com**)

Jennifer Jackson (**http://arcaedia.livejournal.com**)

Jonathon Lyons (**http://lyonsliterary.blogspot.com**)

Lauren MacLeod (**www.strothmanagency.com/articles**)

Holly Root (**http://waxmanagency.wordpress.com**)

Social media

Social media such as LinkedIn[SM], Facebook[SM], and Twitter[SM] provide opportunities to expand your networks, grow your contact list, and learn about the publishing industry.

LinkedIn[SM] (www.linkedin.com)

When you join groups on LinkedIn[SM], you can ask and answer questions and follow discussions on writing, selling, and publishing your book. There are many active writing and publishing groups to consider joining, including:

- **Authors, Writers, Publishers, and Agents Group.** Discussions and literary networking for literary agents, writers, publishers, scriptwriters, and authors.

- **Writing Mafia.** Designed to share information for writers, journalists, copywriters, editors, and authors.

- **Writing Professionals.** A group for professional and aspiring novelists, poets, essayists, journalists, editors, and authors.

- **Book Publishing Professionals.** An international platform for book publishing professionals to share their expertise and resources. Group includes people involved in book sales, marketing, editorial, and production.

- **Authors and Publishers Association.** An education and networking group, open to authors, publishers, book manufacturers, agents, publicists, editors, illustrators, graphic designers, ghostwriters, and all others involved in the literary trade.

- **Authors, Writers, Publishers, Editors, and Other Professionals.** Group open to all professions within the publishing industry with the goal of connecting, networking, and learning from others in the industry.

- **Writing and Editing Professionals.** An international group dedicated to discussing writing and editing.

- **Books Sales and Marketing.** Established to provide networking and education on selling and marketing books. This group is for authors, publishers, editors, book literary agents, and future writers.

- **Association of Writers.** This group is for anyone interested in writing. Members help one another stay focused and share tips for writing, acquiring and working with an agent, and being published.

Twitter^SM (http://twitter.com)

Twitter^SM is about more than telling your followers what you are doing right now in 140 characters or less. Author Matt Stewart promoted his unpublished novel via Twitter^SM and tweeted his way to a book deal. In July 2009, Stewart began tweeting portions of his manuscript, *The French Revolution*. By September 2009, he had built a large enough market and community to attract a publisher. Used effectively, Twitter^SM can garner attention for your writing and platform, and directly connect you with literary agents. Booksquare University (**http://booksquareuniversity.com**) offers a free directory of hundreds of publishing industry professionals, literary agents, and authors to follow, as well as Tweet Camp, a $399 workshop designed to teach writers how to use Twitter^SM to achieve the best results.

Facebook^SM (www.facebook.com)

Facebook^SM is one of the most popular social networking sites. It is an excellent resource for writers as it allows personal interaction with other members and offers a live feed application to share blog posts, news, links, published articles, and Twitter^SM updates in real time.

The Association of Author's Representatives

The Association of Author's Representatives (AAR) consists of reputable, experienced literary agents. To become a member, agents must have sold 18 books within ten months and adhere to strict ethical guidelines. The AAR Web site (**www.AAR-Online.org**) provides a list of members and information on how to contact them.

Identify the literary agent of a book

If you want to know who the agent was for a particular book, examine the acknowledgements page to find the author's agent. Writers tend to thank their literary agents, and it is a good way to locate the agent for a specific author. Other ways to identify the literary agent for a book:

- Use a search engine and insert the author's name and the term "literary agent."

- Use Google™ book search: **www.books.google.com**. In the search box, type in the name of the agent in quotation marks, followed by the word "acknowledgements." Alternatively, type in the name of the book in quotation marks, and then the word "acknowledgements." The search results should lead you to the acknowledgements pages of books listing the searched agent, or in the case of the latter search, the acknowledgements page for the particular book.

- If all else fails, telephone the publisher directly and ask the receptionist for the editor who worked on the book. If you are lucky, you will be transferred to the editor's assistant. Unfortunately, more often than not, your call will be transferred into a sort of telephone limbo zone. If you do reach the editor's assistant, politely request the name of the acting literary agent for the book.

Writers' organizations

Many writers' organizations have newsletters, meetings, events, and Web sites that provide information about agents. *A list of professional writers' organizations can be found in Appendix II.*

Magazines

You can find the names of literary agents in writer's magazines, such as *The Writer, Writer's Digest,* and *Poets & Writers,* which publish articles about agents as well as articles written by agents.

Media exposure

It is the rare occasion that a literary agent will seek out an author and offer to represent him, but it does happen. You have a chance of attracting the attention of a literary agent if:

- You self-publish your book and it sells tens of thousands of copies.

- Your fiction writing wins a prestigious award or contest.

- Your writing garners extensive media coverage in literary journals or well-respected online outlets.

RESEARCHING AGENTS

Each agent has different skills, experience, strengths, and specific types of writing he represents. Prior to approaching and pitching an agent, you need to carefully conduct research to determine which ones are the best fit for your style, personality, needs, and genre. The directories, databases, associations, and Web sites listed above will help you collect the information you need to systematically assess prospective agents.

Questions to consider when evaluating an agent:

- **How important is an agent's experience?** An effective agent is one who has established strong contacts with publishers and editors, understands how to negotiate contracts and sell subsidiary rights, and who can work well with writers. Much of this knowledge and skill is acquired through experience, but that does not mean a newer agent is not effective. Many newer agents have a background in editing or book sales, or experience working as assistants to agents. New agents are in the process of building their clientele and are more open to new writers and new ideas, and they have more time to devote to selling books and will work harder to establish sales.

- **Would you prefer to work with a large, medium, or small agency?** Most agencies are small agencies consisting of one or two agents. There are approximately 100 medium-size agencies with three to six people on staff, and 20 large agencies made up of eight or more agents. The prestigious large agencies include: Writers House, William Morris,

Curtis Brown, International Creative Management, Janklow & Nesbit Associates, and Sterling Lord Literistic. Large and small agencies offer different benefits. Large agencies have a full staff: accountants to track payments and disburse funds; attorneys to negotiate contracts; agent assistants to accept your calls when the agent is unavailable; subsidiary rights specialists to sell film serial, and foreign rights; and publicists to promote your platform. Large agencies focus on commercial properties with additional revenue potential.

Small agencies tend to be more receptive to first-time writers and projects that are less profitable. They are more accessible, easier to reach, and usually respond quicker to queries. You may also find they value and nurture quality relationships with their writers.

- **Does the agent represent fiction or nonfiction and does the agent represent your specific subcategory within your genre?** Many agents represent either fiction or nonfiction (though some represent both) and specific categories within those genres. An agent may represent historical romance novels, but not contemporary romance fiction. Another agent may deal with practical nonfiction, such as business, fitness, and parenting, but not handle narrative nonfiction, such as biography, history, or investigative journalism. Some agents represent literary fiction exclusively and others prefer commercial fiction. It is essential to only approach agents who represent your genre and subcategory. You should have a clear understanding of your type of writing so you do not waste time pitching agents who will not be interested in your manuscript or book idea.

- **How many deals has the agent made in his or her career?** An agent who has sold two books has less experience and sales ability than an agent who has sold 200 books. You want an agent that can land you a book deal. Unless the agent is new to the industry and just starting out (and you; therefore, expect him or her to have a lower number of book sales), then the better choice is the agent who has the higher sales rate.

- **How many deals has she brokered recently?** The publishing industry rewards what you have done lately, not what you have accomplished in the past. You want an agent who is currently active. An agent who has only sold 25 books in her career, but 15 of them were sold in the past year, may be a better choice for representation than an agent who has sold 200 books in her career, but only sold one within the last 12 months.

- **What kind of publishers has he or she brokered deals with?** Has the agent brokered deals mainly with small publishers or large publishers? Are most of the sales with the same publisher or the same type of publisher, such as academic presses? Ideally, you want to work with an agent who brokers most sales with major publishers. Major publishers pay higher advances, print more copies of your book, acquire the best distribution, and have larger promotional budgets.

- **What kinds of advances has the agent negotiated?** Advances vary widely depending on the type of book, which publisher bought it, and the size of the author's platform. A typical advance for a first-time writer may be $15,000 to $20,000 per book. If the agent you are considering consistently acquires advances that are less than the typical rate, he or she may lack experience or negotiating skills.

- **Do you recognize the authors the agent represents?** If you are assessing the viability of a new agent, you may not recognize the names of the authors she represents. However, if the agent is well established, you should know a few of the writers on his or her client list.

- **Are you a good match for the agent's client list?** Are the agent's clients synergistic with you and your work? Does she represent books that have a similar subject matter or style as yours? The agent may be a good fit if she represents a majority of new writers or authors within your same genre. On the other hand, if all the agent's clients are established, bestselling authors, and you are a first-time writer, then the agent probably is not the right match.

- **Is the agent receptive to new clients and new writers?** You need an agent who is actively looking for new clients. An agent who has been in the business for ten years may not be accepting new clients. As a general rule, a newer agent — one with three or less years of experience — will be more receptive to garnering first-time writers.

CREATING AN AGENT FILE

Once you have found the agents you are interested in approaching and have sorted through the information, you will need to organize your research. Creating an agent file will help you design a systematic plan to approach your target agents. The goal is to divide and rank your preselected list of agents into categories based on your prerequisites, so you can narrow down your options and make informed decisions about the best agents to approach.

You can create your file system with a computer spreadsheet or with simple manila folders. Use as many or as few files and categories as necessary for your particular needs, and order them based on your priorities. For instance, if your goal is to acquire an agent at a large firm, who has less than three years experience, has sold a minimum of 35 books in his or her career, most of which were sold in the past 12 months, negotiates strong advances for clients, is a member of the AAR, and specializes in urban fantasy romance – the agents that have most of these characteristics would be filed in your "Group One" folder. You might decide that agents who have most of these qualifications, but work in smaller agencies will be filed in your "Group Two" folder. You may place agents that meet these requirements, but are not yet members of AAR in your "Group Three" folder.

Once you have thoroughly organized your research and prioritized your target agent list, you can effectively and efficiently begin the pitch process. The next section of this book covers what is included in the pitch package, how to successfully create the necessary components, and how to submit your pitch for the best results.

CASE STUDY: "HOW I ACQUIRED MY AGENT"

Carrie Wilson Link
Web site – www.carriewilsonlink.com
Blog – http://fully-caffeinated.blog-spot.com

Books: *UNSTRUNG: Memoir of a Mended Marriage*

Genre: Memoir

I know many published writers: They all said, "You need an agent." They explained that an agent does not just sell the book for you, but also represents you through the contract process. I felt I needed someone to do that for me.

An agent I knew who was not taking on new clients, gave me a list of agent friends of hers and graciously allowed me to use her name when querying them, so I knew that at least those query letters would get read.

I bought a book on how to write book proposals and followed the instructions. As a memoir writer, I also had to have my manuscript completed before pitching to agents. I continued to build my platform through my blog, which currently receives more than 10,000 hits each month, and using social networking sites like Facebook[SM] to grow my networks.

I approached 22 agents before acquiring one. Six weeks after receiving my query, I got an e-mail from one, apologizing for taking so long. She explained she had just gone through a "surprise divorce." I knew right away she was someone I would like: honest, real, and human. I then sent her the manuscript, the proposal, and a typed letter explaining what I had to offer as a writer and what I was looking for in an agent. I also sent her a copy of my favorite book, *SPLIT: Memoir of a Divorce,* which is about a "surprise divorce." I explained that Suzanne Finnamore was a favorite author of mine and that our writing styles are similar. I wrote this in a personal note and mailed it. The rest is history.

Finding the right agent takes a while, but the wait is worth it — you do not just want any agent, you want one you really click with. For me, it was important to meet my agent in person. We spent the better part of two days together and I would not trade that experience for the world. Plus, I now have seen with my own eyes just how crazy her job is.

SECTION 2:
Submitting the Pitch

The Pitch Package

ow that you have compiled and prioritized your agent file you are ready to begin approaching agents. There are standard procedures and guidelines for pitching agents. Depending on the type of books you write, the pitch package may consist of:

- The query letter

- The book proposal

- The synopsis

- The manuscript

After the initial query, if an agent is interested in your project then he or she will request additional material.

- *If you write fiction* — the agent will request a synopsis and your complete manuscript.

- *If you write narrative nonfiction* — the agent will request a book proposal and your complete manuscript.

- *If you write practical nonfiction* — the agent will request a book proposal and sample chapters.

UNDERSTANDING THE ELEMENTS OF THE PITCH PACKAGE

To effectively capture the attention of a literary agent you must have a full understanding of the elements of the pitch package. Each component of the pitch package is explained in detail in the following chapters; however, an overview of each element. *The query letter is covered in Chapter 6, the book proposal in Chapter 7, the synopsis in Chapter 8, and the manuscript in Chapter 9.* Below is an.

The query letter

Your initial sales pitch to an agent will be in the form of a one-page query letter. The query letter is your opportunity to grab the agent's attention and motivate him to ask for the book proposal or manuscript. The goal of the query is to intrigue the agent with your book idea or story and get him to consider representing you. *Examples of successful query letters are included in Appendix VII.*

The book proposal

The book proposal is a marketing tool used to sell a nonfiction book idea. Publishers commission nonfiction books to be written. In other words, the author does not write the book until *after* a publisher has agreed to publish it. Nonfiction writers land a book deal based on an idea for a book, which is presented in the book proposal, and one to three sample chapters. *A full example of a book proposal is included in Appendix IX.*

The synopsis

Agents who initially only request a few chapters of a novel will also ask for a synopsis. The synopsis summarizes your entire story detailing the events and characters. Some agents will request that writers submit the synopsis along with the query letter. *Examples of successful synopses are included in Appendix VII.*

The manuscript

Writers of fiction and narrative nonfiction must have a completed and polished manuscript prior to approaching an agent. Agents do not accept pitches for ideas for novels or memoirs; they do not accept pitches for *almost finished* manuscripts; they accept pitches for ready-to-market books.

APPROACHING AGENTS

Acquiring an agent has as much to do with thorough research as it does with approaching a high number of agents. The more agents you approach, the better chance you have of successfully finding an agent. Your agent file should have a minimum of 40 to 50 agents to approach, each ranked in order of their desirability based on your specific requirements.

To make the submission process manageable, you will want to divide your list into groups of eight to ten agents to approach. So if you have a list of 40 agents divided into groups of eight, you will have five groups of agents to approach. Approach your dream agents in "Group One" first. If you do not land an agent in the first round of submissions, do not become discouraged — simply go on to the next set of eight to ten agents to pitch.

Create a file to keep track of when each agent was contacted, when you expect to receive a response, the result of the response, and any follow-up notes. It should not take any longer than four weeks to receive an initial response to your query letter. If you have not received a response from an agent within one month, and he or she is one of your 'dream' agents, consider submitting a brief follow-up note. If you still do not receive a response, move on to the next set of agents to query.

Simultaneous submissions

Submitting query letters to more than one agent at the same time is standard practice in the literary world, and it benefits the writer. An agent may take two to four weeks to review your query letter and respond. The response will either be a rejection letter or a request for further material, in which case the agent will need an additional four to eight weeks to review the manuscript or proposal. If you only query one agent at a time, it could take years to find an agent. Querying multiple agents simultaneously should land you an agent within six months, as long as you are approaching the right agents (which you should be based on your extensive research) and pitching them effectively (which you will be able to do with the knowledge you gained from reading this book).

THE SUBMISSION PROCESS

Always follow guidelines

It is imperative to follow each agent's submission guidelines. You can find agent's specific guidelines on their Web sites, and in their online and print directory listings. Agents say the chief reason they reject a submission is due to the writer not following the guidelines. Why risk having your query discarded or dismissed because of a technicality? It is easy to follow instructions and will greatly increase the chance your query will be considered. It shows you have taken the initiative to research the agent and are conscientious of the agent's time, tastes, and needs. Many agents feel a writer who cannot follow directions during the pitching process will be a difficult client, so they will not even bother reading the pitch.

Requests for exclusivity

If an agent is interested in your project, he or she may ask to read your manuscript or book proposal on an exclusive basis. A request for exclusivity means the agent wants to be the only one allowed to read and consider your work. The agent is asking that you do not share your novel or proposal with any other agent. This can create a dilemma for an author, as it will put the submission process on hold. However, receiving an exclusivity request is a positive sign that an agent is serious about representing you.

Most writers handle requests for exclusivity by placing a limit on the time the agent has to review the material, so they are not waiting indefinitely for a response or holding up subsequent requests from other interested agents. Let the agent know that you are giving him or her exclusivity for a set period of time, usually two to four weeks for a book proposal or six to eight weeks for a manuscript. If during the exclusive time period you receive a request to review your book proposal or manuscript from another agent you queried, you will have to wait until the exclusive time period is over before sending your material to the next agent. The best policy is to be honest and explain the situation.

Submitting via e-mail

Many agents prefer to receive submissions via e-mail. Here are tips to follow when submitting your pitch online:

- If possible, e-mail the agent directly instead of submitting your query to the general agency mailbox. If you cannot locate the agent's direct e-mail address on the agency's Web site, you may find it at Publishers Marketplace. Otherwise, call the agency and ask the receptionist for the agent's e-mail address.

- Maintain a formal presentation. Just because you are sending an e-mail does not mean it should become a casual, personal note. Keep your query letter businesslike and address the agent appropriately.

- Unless otherwise specified in the agent's submission guidelines, your query letter should be contained in the body of the e-mail. Do not include attachments. Most agents will automatically delete an e-mail that contains an attachment.

- Limit your query letter to one page. Queries are meant to be only one page in length, regardless of whether you are submitting it via e-mail or snail mail. Resist the temptation to write a pitch that is longer than the accepted standard. To ensure the query adheres to the equivalent of one paper page, copy and paste it into a word document. If it exceeds one page length, you need to shorten it.

- Do not simply send an e-mail note to an agent asking the agent to visit a link to your Web site or blog to learn more about you and your project. That is not a query and will be ignored.

- Ensure the subject line identifies the content of the e-mail or includes wording requested by the agent. For instance, some agents state that e-mail queries should contain the subject line "query," or "novel query," or "nonfiction query."

- Do not use all caps or all lower case typing in your query or subject line. Use proper punctuation and grammar.

E-mail formatting

The body of an e-mail does not retain formatting. What may look professional on your computer may be incomprehensible gibberish when received by another computer. An agent may not even be reading your query on a computer — he or she may be viewing it on a cell phone with e-mail capabilities, which strips away e-mail formatting altogether. Here are tips for formatting a query letter, sample pages, synopsis, or book proposal when submitting via e-mail:

- Turn off the formatting in your e-mail program. Do not use bold, italics, underline, special fonts, nonstandard sizes, or colors.

- Single-space text for less than five pages of content. Double-space the text if it is more than five pages in length.

- Do not indent a paragraph.

- Use an extra space between each paragraph.

- Do not mark your e-mail as high priority.

- Do not include attachments of any kind.

- E-mail your query to yourself before sending it to the agent, to ensure the text is readable.

Submitting via standard mail

Few agents still accept query letters via snail mail. However, some experts believe that pitches submitted by mail are viewed as more important than e-mail queries and have an increased chance of receiving serious consideration. If an agent accepts submissions by standard mail and e-mail, or if the agent does not specify the method of submission, then submit your pitch using regular mail. Here are tips to follow when submitting your query by mail:

- Include an SASE (self addressed stamped envelope). Agents receive thousands of queries each year. They cannot afford the time it takes to address envelopes to each writer or the cost of postage for each response letter that needs to be sent. If you do not include an SASE, your chances of receiving a response are slim.

- Be sure to include your complete contact information in your letter so the agent may contact you via telephone or e-mail if he or she chooses.

- Double-check the agency's mailing address and the spelling of the agent's name.

- Use standardized, plain white paper and a white envelope.

What not to do when submitting your pitch:

- Never send sample pages, a complete manuscript, or your book proposal with your query letter unless the agent's guidelines specifically request them. Some writers believe that since they are pitching the agent anyway, they might as well submit samples of their writing along with their query letter, and the agent will be so impressed with their manuscript or pages that it will make the difference in landing representation. It will make a difference — by landing the writer's submission in the trash. Agents barely have time to read a one-page query letter; therefore, if they receive unsolicited pages or a complete manuscript, that submission goes at the bottom of the pile to be read last, or worse, to never be read at all.

- Do not call the agent to pitch your idea, to inform that you are sending the query, or to ask if the agent received your query. An agent will consider such behavior too aggressive. Agents want clients who will be easy to work with, not writers who will be pushy and demanding of their time.

- Do not show up at the agent's office unannounced. Dropping off a query letter in person is probably the worst thing a writer can do to sabotage his chances of acquiring an agent. Always adhere to the agent's submission guidelines. Violating requests or exhibiting aggressive behavior turns agents off.

- Do not include gifts with your submission. Including an object that ties in with your book's theme may seem like a good idea, but it is not. Do not send a pen engraved with the title of your book, or a cupcake along with your pitch for a dessert cookbook, or a packet of seeds representing the garden in your romance novel. These items will not help differentiate you from the crowd. Instead, they make a writer appear gimmicky, amateur, and desperate.

- Do not use fancy stationary. The publishing industry is a business. Agents want to know the author understands this. Always maintain a professional, businesslike presentation.

CASE STUDY: EXPERT ADVICE FROM LITERARY AGENT BARBARA POELLE

```
Irene Goodman Literary Agency
27 West 24th Street, Suite 700B
New York, New York 10010
Web site - www.irenegoodman.com
queries@irenegoodman.com
```

Agency's books and authors include: *The New York* Times bestsellers *Seduction Becomes Her* by Shirless Busbee and *Devil In My Bed* by Celeste Bradley, and a USA Today Bestseller *The Girl Most Likely To* by Susan Donovan.

On how to find an agent: You find an agent the same way you would write a book: research, research, and research. There are so many viable sources in every media these days that a big red flag starts waving if you are sending me a children's book or Christian literature when my profile clearly states I am looking for thrillers, mysteries, historical romances, and humorous nonfiction. I probably can't trust your work to have much attention to detail.

On what she looks for in fiction manuscripts: I look for a unique take on an existing formula buoyed by a solid execution that grabs me by the ears and stuffs me into the pages. Let's face it, there aren't really any new plots, but there are always new stories.

On what makes a good query letter: Three things: The Hook, The Book, and The Cook. You should be able to tell me about your book in a succinct sentence — this is the "hook" — which may also be referred to as a "log line" (for instance, "A great white shark terrorizes a small New England beach town over 4th of July weekend"). Then you should expand the description into five or six sentences — which is the "book" — and can also be used as an "elevator pitch," meaning a verbal pitch when meeting agents, editors, and the basic public face to face. This section of the written query should also have the word count as well as the current comparative titles on the shelf. (And for the love of all that's holy, don't say J.K. Rowling or Stephen King). And finally, the "cook" — which is you, and it doesn't matter if you have zero publishing credits — just be able to state in the cook section *why this book, why you and why now.*

On what she looks for in nonfiction book proposals: I'm looking for platform. How many people are already excited about your book? I wish I could tell you that a good story or an interesting topic will always cross the finish line victorious, but in today's media-driven world, there must be evidence of staying power; having a solid online presence or growing multimedia platform is like stapling a golden ticket to the proposal.

On paying attention to trends: I say treat your novel the way you live: with 98 percent passion and 2 percent common sense. Pay attention to trends, but write what you're passionate about.

Query letter mistakes to avoid: The mistakes people make in queries are so numerous and hilarious that they themselves could make up an entire book. (Hmm, now there's an idea, anybody know an agent?) Poorly executed queries vary from misinformed to outright insulting and before we went electronic, they might also arrive with "gifts" ranging from homemade food products to bedazzled soda cozies.

Tips for maintaining a good working relationship: Like any relationship, respect is the cornerstone. There needs to be a great deal of trust and enthusiasm on both sides of the table, but above all, the understanding that this is a business venture and everybody wants the results to be wildly successful. I absolutely adore my clients; I find them to be as delightfully different as their genres, but what they all have in common is a great deal of focus and patience in an industry that demands both.

GETTING TO "YES"

Agents want clients they can work with throughout the authors' careers. Here are ten things you can do to increase the chance an agent will say, "yes" to your initial pitch:

1. Ensure the first line of your pitch shows that you have done your research. Do not pitch a children's book to an agent who specializes in historical romance.

2. Let the agent know why you are approaching him or her specifically.

3. Tailor each pitch to the target agent. Never send a query to an agency. An author hires an individual agent, not an agency.

4. Be polite, not demanding.

5. Be willing to work with the agent on edits that will improve your chances of landing a book deal.

6. Present a tightly focused story or proposal. The tighter the focus of the book, the wider the potential audience. Agents do not want authors who try to be all things to everyone.

7. Be impeccably professional.

8. Show you are determined to be a successful author, are willing to put forth the effort necessary to make it happen, and have a plan to do so.

9. Have a compelling idea for a series of books as opposed to one book.

10. Convey that you understand the publishing industry and what is expected of you.

CASE STUDY: "HOW I ACQUIRED MY AGENT":

Billy Coffey
Web site - www.billycoffey.com
Blog: www.billycoffey.com/blog

Books: Snow Day (Faithwords, 2010)

Genre: Spiritual Memoir

Agent: Rachelle Gardner, WordServe Literary

I had done enough research to know that most, if not all, of the larger publishers required submissions to come through an agent. I queried more than 30 agents and got the standard "No thanks" from all of them. Not because the book was bad, but because I did not have a platform. I needed to build an online presence. I started a blog, which was much easier said than done. There are literally millions of blogs out there, and gaining an audience is no small feat. But I kept at it, read and commented on other blogs, and used

Facebook and especially Twitter to connect with other people. It worked. I had a new reader stumble upon my blog, who was represented by Rachelle Gardner, and she asked me if I had considered submitting my work to her and offered to let me use her name. The query letter is an absolute horror to write. I think I spent more time on that than I did the last draft of my manuscript. I studied what Rachelle wanted in an initial submission and made sure to stick to that, offering no more and no less. Along with most other agents, she rejects many queries because writers fail to abide by that one simple rule. Within a week, she requested my proposal and full manuscript.

I also followed Rachelle's guidelines when revising my proposal. She was very clear on what she wanted, and I made it a point to oblige her. A proposal is the most important document you will write other than the book itself. Not only will your agent see it, but it is also what is passed around from publisher to publisher. It has to be as flawless as you can make it, and you have to do your research. In this age, marketing and competing titles are an essential part of any proposal, and I made sure those were especially strong.

As for my manuscript, I wrote and rewrote and rewrote again, and then passed it along to trusted friends who I could count on to tear it apart sentence by sentence. It is difficult for a writer to look at his or her work as a Thing rather than a representation of himself. Cutting a paragraph or a chapter can feel like self-mutilation, but it is always better if you do it yourself rather than an editor.

Within a few weeks I had an agent. I had been an avid reader of Rachelle's blog for a long time, and it was obvious she was both respected in the publishing world and a nice person. We spoke on the phone about what we both wanted from my book. I knew then she was the right agent for me.

Rachelle had me tweak a few small things with my proposal. She is an amazing editor, and we went through my book and managed to cut 10,000 words to make it a bit easier to read. In the end, it is the publishing editor who needs to think of any reason why your manuscript is not a fit for the house — it is the nature of the business. Rachelle wanted to ensure that the manuscript did not offer any of those reasons. Two weeks later, she brokered a book deal with a publisher.

What I have learned from the process is that agents truly are people enamored with the art of writing. Agents are always looking out for the next big find. Despite the aggravations, they enjoy their work and they want everyone to succeed. Agents suffer right along with the writers they represent. Every rejection one of their writers receive is also their own, and the disappointment is just as great.

Give them the room to do their job, and concentrate on yours.

Crafting the Query Letter

S mall to mid-size agencies receive an average of 10,000 query letters each year. With a rejection rate of 99 percent, it is imperative that you carefully construct your query to receive a positive response. To achieve this, you must:

- Know your manuscript or book idea well.

- Understand where your book fits in the marketplace.

- Recognize what you have to offer as the writer.

The query letter is an art form unto itself. Following are the components necessary to construct a good query letter, tips to write an effective query, and samples of successful pitches.

COMPONENTS OF THE QUERY LETTER

The query letter is your one-page sales pitch. It must:

- Show the agent that you are capable of quality writing.

- Create excitement for your topic or story.

- Be succinct – providing the information in as few as words as possible.

- Convey that you are a professional author who understands what an agent wants.

Query letters consist of four main components:

- The opening hook

- The supporting details

- The writer's qualifications

- The wrap-up

The opening hook

The first paragraph needs to do two things: Establish a connection with the agent and establish the project.

Establish a connection with the agent

The first sentence of the query letter should explain why you are contacting the particular agent. Possible connections might be:

- **You read a book the agent wrote or an interview in a magazine.** "I recently read your interview in *Writer's Digest* magazine, where I learned you enjoy good barbecue. Because of your culinary desires, I thought you might be interested in my cookbook, GOURMET SOUTHERN COOKING…"

- **You met the agent at a conference or literary event.** "Thank you for speaking with me at Book Expo America last week about my western adventure novel…"

- **The agent represents a similar author and genre.** "I am a loyal John Grisham fan. I could not put down his novel *The Client,* and actually read the entire book in one day. When I learned you were the agent for this magnificent legal thriller, I knew I wanted to query you about my own 82,000-word book, NO JUSTICE ON THE DELTA."

- **You discovered the agent's listing in a directory.** "I found your listing in Writer's Market and feel I may be a good fit for the type of writing you represent…"

- **An associate, friend, or client referred you to the agent by.** "Your author-client, Jane Meadows, referred me to you. Jane is part of my romance novel reading group and a great supporter of my writing, in particular my most recent manuscript, KISS AND TELL…"

Establish the project

In one sentence, briefly introduce the topic or genre, the title, and the length of the book, so the agent understands what the project is.

"EVER FIERCE IN MY HEART is an 85,000-word historical romance set in 1715 London."

"MURDER ON MAIN STREET is a 96,000-word present-day, true crime narrative."

"HOW TO STAGE YOUR HOME TO SELL is a 65,000-word practical, how-to book."

The supporting details

This section expands upon the story or topic. It may take one or two paragraphs. For nonfiction writers, the supporting details may include how the research will be conducted and how the information will be gathered, who will be interviewed, the theories that will be presented, who will read the book (the reader demographic), why the book is important or timely, and an overview of the content. For fiction writers, the supporting details section is a summary of the story, presenting the protagonist, his or her dilemma or conflict, the choice the hero makes, and the consequences of that decision.

The writer's qualifications

The next paragraph explains why you are qualified to write the book. This section of the query letter provides an opportunity to impress the agent with your credentials or platform. You might mention the size of your blog readership, the number of speaking engagements you participate in each year, or that you host a popular weekly national radio program. If you have educational degrees, career experience, or publishing credentials, you may include those in this paragraph. Memberships in organizations, articles you have written, a list of media experience, and any contests or awards you have won should be presented.

The wrap-up

The final sentence or two are used to thank the agent for reading your query and request permission to submit additional material.

"Thank you for your time and consideration. I have a two-page and eight-page synopsis available and a completed manuscript for your review."

"Thank you for considering my book idea. May I send you my completed book proposal and two sample chapters?"

QUERY FORMATTING RULES

- The query letter is one page, single-spaced.

- Use Times New Roman font, 12-point.

- The title of your book is written in all caps.

For hard copy letters

- The query letter should be printed on plain letterhead or on plain paper with your name and full contact information including address, telephone, and e-mail, centered at the top of the letter.

- The first line is the date, left justified.

- Skip a line after the date, and insert the agent's name and contact information, left justified.

- Skip a line, and insert the salutation: Dear [agent's name].

- Paragraphs in the body of the letter are indented.

- Use 1-inch margins all around.

For e-mail queries

- The first line is the date.

- Skip a line after the date and insert the salutation: Dear [agent name].

- Paragraphs in the body of the letter are not indented. There is a line of space between paragraphs.

- Your full contact information, including mailing address and telephone number, is listed at the close of the letter.

- The subject line should indicate what is included in the e-mail, for instance "Query Mystery Novel."

- Use an e-mail address that is professional and easy to remember. If possible, simply use your name, such as yourname@emailaddress.com.

12 TIPS FOR WRITING AN EFFECTIVE NONFICTION QUERY LETTER

Nonfiction queries must focus on the writer's platform and potential market for the book. Below are 12 tips for capturing the agent's interest.

1. **Create a catchy title and introduce it early in the query letter.** Succinct, memorable titles help sell books. Show the agent you know how to write and market by crafting an appealing title. Nonfiction titles are usually five words or less. Some books use subtitles to be more descriptive, such as *The Worst Hard Time: The Untold Story of Those Who Survived The Great American Dust Bowl* and *The Devil In The White City: Murder, Magic, and Madness at the Fair That Changed America.* Self-help and how-to book titles need to identify and solve the reader's problem, such as *What to Expect When You're Expecting,* and *How To Solve Your Credit Problem Now.* An effective exercise is to come up with ten to 20

titles for your book and ask friends, family, and associates to vote on which one they like best.

2. **Show why the book is timely.** Note any trends or media exposure that indicates a growing popularity in your subject. You do not need to find a current hot topic and craft your book idea around it, you just need to find a timely factor, such as a new study, a recent article, or a popular trend to help support your pitch.

3. **Convince the agent that you have a target market.** Citing statistics of your potential readership shows that you understand your market niche. If you have an idea for a book about home schooling and you can quote a U.S. Department of Education report, which forecasts the number of families who plan to home school their children in the next two to five years, that would be an effective statistic to include in your query and would indicate that you have a target market.

4. **Include other possible sales potentials.** If the director of an annual festival or convention has agreed to purchase 4,000 copies of your book for next year's event, or a university plans to make it a requirement for one of its ongoing classes, then be sure to convey that sales potential in your pitch.

5. **Narrow the idea for greatest impact.** A narrowly focused nonfiction book sells better than a broad-based one and agents are looking for narrowly defined ideas. There are hundreds of books available on the topic of home schooling. If you plan to write about home schooling, you will need to sharply focus the content of the book. Instead of *Home Schooling for Everyone*, you might write about *Home Schooling Teenage Boys*, or *Art Projects for Home Schooling*, or *Home Schooling Assignments while Traveling in Europe*.

6. **List possible spin-offs or series ideas for the book.** If your book idea lends itself easily to additional books, then note that in the query letter. If your book idea is *Home Schooling for Teenage Boys*, possible spin-offs might be *Home Schooling for Teenage Girls*, and *Home Schooling for First-Graders*. A series of books might include *Home Schooling for Teenage Boys: The Sciences; Home Schooling for Teenage Boys: Literature;* and *Home Schooling for Teenage Boys: History*.

7. **Differentiate your book.** Impress the agent by conducting thorough research and presenting information to show why your book is needed. Know what other books are available and outline why your book is different from others already on the market. Perhaps other books on the topic are out-of-date, or lack information you will provide, or present a different viewpoint. Or maybe the book is needed because no other books exist on the subject.

8. **Be realistic.** Publishers expect certain types of nonfiction books to be written by experts. If you are not a psychologist, doctor, or attorney, it is not realistic that you will be selected to write a serious book about medicine, psychiatry, or legal matters. You might have a chance at authoring pop culture books on those topics, but not serious studies on those subjects. Most biographies and histories are written by experienced journalists or scholars, and in the case of celebrity tell-alls, a former confidant, or associate. So unless you are Britney Spears' ex-best friend, a Harvard professor, or a seasoned investigative reporter for *The New York Times*, you most likely will not be writing a book on any of these topics. Your query must present a realistic idea that you can realistically write.

9. **Include adequate details.** You want the agent to have a full picture of your book idea so he can effectively consider requesting your complete proposal. A book titled *Home Schooling Teenage Boys* needs to convey more information than that it is a book about schooling teenage boys at home. Will the book provide practical solutions or be exclusively theoretical? Will it include sample assignments? Will it be written for moms, or for dads, or for both parents to read? Will it be written in a casual tone, a humorous style, or in a straight academic manner? What material and subjects will it cover? A query letter does not include every detail about the book (that is what the book proposal is for), but it should provide enough details to arouse interest and allow the agent to make an informed decision regarding requesting additional material.

10. **Drop names if you have them.** If you have an association or connection with a celebrity, an academic, a noted author, or an authority on your subject who has agreed to write a book blurb, quote, or the foreword, it is a selling point and should be included in your query letter.

11. **List three to five things you will do to promote the book.** Platform is key to securing a literary agent for a nonfiction book. Your promotional list should include substantial items, such as contacting your network of 50,000 followers, mentioning the book each week on your national radio show, conducting a blog and social media book tour, and distributing a series of professional produced training videos (that are tied to your book) to online video outlets.

12. **Mention self-published books only if they sold well.** Because anyone can publish a book using today's technology, agents do not view self-published books seriously. They may believe that the book was self-published because the quality was poor, it was badly written, or it was just not good enough to garner a traditional publisher. It is best only to mention a self-published book if it sold several thousand copies, received noted media attention, or won a prestigious award.

Considerations for practical nonfiction books

Practical nonfiction writers must demonstrate they can explain terms, concepts, and steps and guide the reader to a destination or goal. How-to and self-help books can take many forms, so you must be specific in your pitch about your format by explaining the general layout of the book, for instance if you will include sidebars, case studies, interviews, Q&As, anecdotes, illustrations, charts, instructions, or quizzes. If you are not an expert on the subject you plan to write about, you will also need to mention the experts that you will use as sources.

Considerations for narrative nonfiction books

Narrative nonfiction pitches must convey the voice, style, tone, and point of view of the completed manuscript. Use the query letter to immerse the reader in the story by synopsizing the plot or opening the pitch with a dynamic excerpt. Provide a summary of where the book will 'take' the reader including what feelings it will evoke, the scope of the story, the conflict, the dilemma, the protagonist and antagonist, and the ultimate lesson.

EIGHT TIPS FOR CREATING AN EFFECTIVE FICTION QUERY LETTER

Along with the previous defined elements of a query letter, fiction pitches need to focus on delivering a captivating summary and dealing with the question of credentials for writers who may not have an established platform.

1. **Create a hook.** Capture the agent's interest by creating a two-to-three sentence hook that introduces the protagonist and the premise. "Fourteen-year-old Wyatt Walker grew up on the run working alongside his dad, a covert spy for the CIA. Wyatt learned the art of karate, how to hide out undercover, use advanced surveillance equipment and weapons, and speak five languages. Now his father has retired to a sleepy little town on the banks of New Orleans and Wyatt must adjust to a life he has never known — one of a normal teenage kid."

2. **Deliver a captivating synopsis.** A pitch for a novel should give the agent a sense of the completed book. After presenting the hook, deliver a one- to two-paragraph synopsis that touches on the main elements of the story. Highlight important characters, the antagonist, emotional turning points, the conflict or dilemma, the climax and the final lesson.

3. **Leave the agent wanting more.** End with a "teaser" that leaves the agent wanting to know what happens next in the story, for example, leave the agent wondering "What will happen to Mary when her partner learns she is a double-agent?"

4. **Show, do not tell.** You want to show the agent your story through your writing, not tell the agent that "it is a great story," or that you are "a wonderful writer."

5. **Immediately immerse the agent in the story.** Consider jumping right into the heart of the book and establishing a connection with the agent and providing the logistics of the project after presenting the story synopsis.

6. **Demonstrate the tone and style of the book.** If you have written a thriller, create suspense with your writing. If your novel is a romance,

deliver an emotional punch. If your manuscript is light-hearted, be sure to include humor in your pitch. Also, use present tense and active verbs to convey a sense of immediacy and immersion.

7. **Check the word count.** Ensure the word count is appropriate for your genre and the agent's requirements, You can do so by referring the agent's Web site. *A word count chart was included in Chapter 2.*

8. **Deal with the question of credentials.** For fiction authors, the quality of your writing is what will ultimately land you an agent and sell your book. Regardless of that fact, it is important to include at least a few sentences about your qualifications. If you are struggling with this section of the query letter because you lack previous publishing credentials or awards, consider focusing on your life experience if it relates to your book.

"My ten years experience as a couple's therapist has given me incredible insight into developing characters for my new chick-lit book, AND I WANT A DIVORCE…"

"As a criminal defense attorney for 25 years, I have represented accused jewel thieves and have insider knowledge of what it takes to plan an intricate diamond heist and almost get away with it. This lends my crime novel an air of authenticity…."

"An unwed mother by the age of 17, I have personal experience of what it's like to raise a child while still a child myself. That is why I believe I am the perfect author for…."

Extra Tip: Check out literary agent Janet Reid's witty and informative blog, Query Shark (**www.QueryShark.com**), for analysis of good and bad fiction queries.

DO'S AND DON'TS OF QUERY LETTER WRITING

Below is a checklist compiled from professional agents' requests.

*   ***Do* get to the point.** Agents are busy people. They only have a limited amount of time to consider your project. If you ramble on about non-

consequential things, such as "I spent two months crafting this letter hoping to get it just right after spending six years writing my manuscript. If I do not find an agent soon I think I will just give up and go back to washing dishes at the local diner…" you will alienate the agent. If you cannot write a tight, pertinent pitch, how will you write a succinct book?

- *Do* **follow the correct format and keep the letter to only one page.** The format of your letter demonstrates you are a professional author who understands what is required. A pitch that is longer than one page (or two at the very most) stands a good chance of never being read.

- *Do* **mention that you have queried multiple agents.** It is professional and demonstrates you understand how the business works.

- *Do* **include information about a previously published book if it sold well.** Agents say it is easier to place a debut book than it is a book by an author who has a mixed sales track-record. A previously published book is only an advantage if it sold very well. If it did, then mention it, but keep the focus of the query on your new project.

- *Do not* **compare your work to known authors.** Positioning your book alongside other published works in style, subject, or readership is acceptable, but do not compare the quality of your writing to established authors. For example "Similar in plotting to Clive Barker, but closer in style to Stephen King" is fine. Stating "My writing is as innovative as J.K. Rowling," or "I am the next Seth Godin" will make you appear conceited, not confident. Your writing will speak for itself. There is already one Seth Godin, and there is only one you, so resist comparing yourself and your writing to other authors.

- *Do not* **send your letter certified mail.** Doing so may annoy the agent.

- *Do not* **discuss money, contracts, or film deals.** Doing so makes you appear amateurish and aggressive. Your job at this point is to capture the agent's interest for your work. Payment, royalties, subsidiary rights, and other contract details are negotiated once a publisher makes an offer to purchase your book.

- *Do not* **introduce yourself by starting the letter with "My name is…"** Your name is included in your contact information and with your signature.

- *Do not* **use the term "fiction novel."** It is redundant — a professional writer understands literary terminology and knows "fiction" and "novel" mean the same thing.

- *Do not* **use the term "novel" for a nonfiction book.** Novels are exclusively fiction.

- *Do not* **state that you are writing a query or seeking representation.** If an agent is reading your letter he knows it is a query and that you are seeking representation.

- *Do not* **mention that your family and friends love your novel or book idea.** The agent does not care what non-writers think about your book. Your work should speak for itself.

- *Do not* **submit a query letter if you have not finished writing the manuscript or book proposal.** An agent cannot evaluate a project if the manuscript or proposal is not complete and available to review. An agent wants to be able to shop the manuscript or book idea to a publisher immediately and will not wait for you to finish the required material.

- *Do not* **demand that the agent read your work or threaten to take it elsewhere.** Threats and demands immediately identify you as an amateur and someone who will be difficult to work with. Stating in a query letter that if the agent does not take you on as a client he or she will be missing out on the next bestseller does not encourage an agent to consider you as a client, instead it demonstrates how unprofessional the author is and leads to the agent dismissing the pitch completely.

- *Do not* **submit a query that does not fit the agent's requirements for genre, word count, or format.** Do not waste your time, or the agent's, attempting to convince him or her to represent your 115,000-word fantasy sci-fi if he or she does not represent that genre, simply because you think it is a great book. It may be, but agents specialize in specific titles and have cultivated resources and expertise in selling those particular titles — they do not suddenly change their guidelines.

- *Do not* **pitch multiple submissions to an agent.** Simultaneous submissions that query more than one agent at the same time is acceptable protocol, but multiple submissions, pitching more than one project to the same agent at the same time, is considered unprofessional.

CASE STUDY: "HOW I ACQUIRED MY AGENT"

Jan Dunlap
Web site: www.jandunlap.com

Books: *Murder on Warbler Weekend* (North Star Press, 2009), *The Boreal Owl Murder* (North Star Press, 2008), and *Purpose, Passion and God: Awakening to the Deepest Meaning of Life* (Twenty-third Publications, 2006)

Genre: Nonfiction (theology and spirituality), Commercial fiction (humor and mystery).

I have had three books published without an agent, but for my newest project, I wanted to pitch into a national market and realized I needed an agent for those contacts.

I knew I had a strong, polished manuscript. I have a first reader and I have been a professional freelance writer for 30 years. Additionally, I teach college composition, so I have plenty of experience with the written word. I also read constantly in many genres.

I approached about ten agents before finding the right one. None of the rejection letters offered any advice or direction for improvement, so I kept polishing my query letter to make it irresistible. I looked at a list of agents who would be at a local writing conference and chose one of them to pitch, based on her bio. Then I studied the company's Web site and realized I needed to pitch her partner instead, so I did that via e-mail. He called me within hours of receiving my e-mail query and we had a long phone discussion about our spiritual perspectives and professional expectations. I was sure it was 'meant to be.'

Creating the Book Proposal

A book proposal is a marketing tool used to present and sell your nonfiction book idea to a publisher before you write the book. It is the only means for selling a nonfiction book to a commercial publisher.

Writing a book proposal benefits you in several ways: It saves you time and effort, and allows you to receive partial payment prior to writing the full manuscript.

THE PURPOSE OF A BOOK PROPOSAL

Many nonfiction authors mistakenly believe that if they write a full manuscript they can send it off to an agent to be sold to a publisher. But agents and editors do not review nonfiction manuscripts, unless they are narrative nonfiction such as memoir or history. A book proposal is required to sell a nonfiction book. A nonfiction manuscript does not answer the editorial review committee's questions about marketing, competition, production, or the author's platform. A publisher will invest tens of thousands of dollars to develop a book and requires a complete view of the project (which the book proposal provides) prior to making a decision.

What the book proposal does:

- Introduces the topic of your book

- Explains why you are qualified to write the book

- Includes sample chapters showcasing the content and your writing ability

- Provides a market analysis of competitive books

- Contains logistical information about the book, such as the length, delivery, and format (sidebars, expert interviews, photos, and charts)

- Analyzes the market for the book (who will buy your book)

- Presents your platform, marketing, and promotional ideas to help sell the book

Editors and agents are overwhelmed by submissions and must choose the most well-written proposals. Many book proposal submissions are poorly written and/or do not answer the fundamental questions necessary for an editor or agent to make an informed decision. By writing a compelling book proposal, you will have the edge over your competition and be better positioned to have your book published.

THE COMPONENTS OF A BOOK PROPOSAL

The book proposal varies in length from 12 to 40 pages, plus the pages of the sample chapter(s), based on the scope of your specific project. It consists of the following sections:

- The title page

- The proposal table of contents

- The overview

- The market

- Competitive analysis

- The promotional plan

- About the author and platform

- The chapter outline

- Sample chapters

- Supplemental material

The overview

The overview section summarizes what your book is about. It needs to concisely convey what you intend to write and should generate interest in the project.

The book proposal should begin with a strong hook. The opening paragraph must evoke excitement in the reader. Effective leads include an anecdote or case study, an interesting fact or statistic, an appropriate quotation that captures the style and tone of your subject, or a compelling question that provokes thought and consideration.

For the remaining overview section you need to:

- Identify the subject and scope of the book

- Present why the book is important or needed

- Include a brief overview of the production details

List the benefits and the features of your book. Then state why your book is unique or timely. Close the overview section with an outline of the book's:

- Special features — such as sidebars, images, charts, quizzes, case studies, checklists or illustrations

- Structure — an explanation of the parts, chapters, and sections of the book

- Estimated word count or page count — an average printed book page has 250 words

- Estimated delivery — a nonfiction book takes an average of six months to one year to complete

The market

The market for your book refers to the audience. Agents and publishers want to know there is a large targeted group of readers who will purchase the book when it is released. In this section you need to:

- Identify the people who will buy your book

- Provide supporting evidence that demonstrates the market is viable

- Demonstrate the potential for spin-offs or a series of books

- Explain any special sales avenues

Who is the market

It is important to identify a large, targeted, specific group of potential readers who want or need what you plan to write about. Include demographic details, such as gender, age range, education, income, social class, and lifestyle in your description (for instance, "Retired African-American women who have survived breast cancer" or "Teenage girls between the ages of 12 and 14 who struggle with math.") It may be tempting to state that the market for your book is "everyone" or "all women," but in reality very few books attain that level of mass appeal. Books targeted to a specific group of people sell far more copies than non-targeted books, so show an agent and publisher that there is a specific target market for your book. Instead of saying your potential readers are "Guys who like to go hiking with their dogs," present a more detailed description, such as "Adventurous males over 40 who own dogs and enjoy backpacking throughout the western United States."

How large is the market

If the potential market for your book is only 5,000, it will be challenging to find an agent and a traditional publisher for your book. It is essential that your book's market not only be specific and targeted, but also large enough to warrant publication.

- Mention the popularity of similar books.

- Include statistics on the topic to support your claims. For example, "In 2011, the oldest of the baby boomer generation, those born in 1946, will turn 65 years old. Fifty-one percent of them are women, and an estimated 4.6 million of those women are African-American..."

- Cite studies and reports.

- Use magazine and newspaper articles to indicate an increased trend toward your subject. For instance, "According to an article in *The New York Times* in January 2009, green construction is on the rise..."

- Note the number of members belonging to associations, trade groups, and organizations who would be interested in your topic.

There are many resources available to help you determine how many potential readers there are for your subject matter:

- Browse the bestseller lists for similar titles.

- Use Internet search engines to find articles and interesting facts.

- For statistical information, peruse the *American Statistical Index* or *Statistical Source,* available at your local library.

- For statistics on the number of books sold annually in a specific genre, review *The Bowker Annual Library and Book Trade Almanac.*

- Read the *Encyclopedia of Associations* to find membership information on just about any type of organization. Available at most public libraries, this book provides an extensive list of thousands of associations on almost any topic.

- *Directories In Print* provides a comprehensive, annotated listing of more than 10,000 business and industrial directories and guides published in the United States.

Series or spin-off potential

Spin-off or series potential is not mandatory to sell your book idea, but an agent or publisher is more interested in projects that beget more product. Books with spin-off or series potential are considered more valuable than stand-alone books. The Chicken Soup for the Soul series has spawned more than 100 books including *Chicken Soup for the Soul: Power Moms; Chicken Soup for the Military Wife's Soul;* and *Chicken Soup for the Soul: What I Learned From My Dog,* as well as a substantial amount of licensed products from greeting cards to calendars. Think of ways your book could become a series or generate spin-offs.

Special sales avenues

Publishers will distribute your book through the normal channels — large retail bookstore chains and online outlets, such as Amazon.com^{SM} and Barnes and Noble^{SM}. These are considered primary sales avenues. If you can present opportunities for secondary sales avenues — such as via independent local bookstores, specialty retail stores, institution sales, libraries, or educational courses — you increase your chances of landing a book deal.

If you are writing a book about organic food, you could mention the number of small bookstores throughout the country that specialize in cookbooks, retail chains that sell culinary-related products (such as Williams-Sonoma^{SM} and Sur La Table^{SM}), health-food stores, resorts and retreats that focus on fitness and nutrition, universities and community colleges that teach organic cooking classes, or large farmers markets across the country. Be creative and think outside the box for any potential sales avenue that would be a good fit for your book's topic. Your own Web site may also be an avenue for selling the book, so be sure to mention it.

Competitive analysis

The purpose of the competitive analysis section is to convince an agent and publisher that there is room on the bookstore shelf for your book. A competitive analysis consists of reviewing and comparing your book idea to six to 12 other similar books on the market, and demonstrating why your book will be better or different from the competitive titles. The list of books in the competitive analysis section also informs the agent and publisher where you envision your book in the marketplace.

Amazon.com^{SM} is an excellent source for identifying similar books. Go to **www.amazon.com** and enter a keyword search for your book idea. Their search engine will produce a list of current books on your topic you can further research. Review the table of contents (using the "Search Inside This Book" tool) and note the topics addressed in the book. Once you have found the six to 12 most appropriate books for comparison, you will need to either purchase the books or obtain them from your local library.

For each book, read a few chapters and identify the approach, point of view, structure, scope, and style. Also, check the bibliography and note if the sources the author used differ from your list. This may indicate a difference in perspective and material covered.

To create the comparative competitive analysis:

- Begin with a lead that restates the need for your book and why it differs from others on the market.

- Provide an analysis and comparison of each book that includes:

  1. Bibliographical information for the competitive title.

  2. A statement of the competitive book's intentions.

  3. An assessment of how that book's information is presented and how effective the book delivers on its promise.

  4. A few sentences explaining what differentiates your book's goals from the competitive book's aims.

  5. Key points of what your book will offer that is more useful or interesting than the other book (remember, you want to critique the book, but do not directly insult the writer or the book).

- Conclude the section by summarizing why your book is better than the other titles.

The promotional plan

The promotional plan details what you will do to help sell the book. Agents and publishers want to know you are willing and capable of marketing the book by evaluating your plan, your platform, and your connections. Your promotional plan may also provide the publishing house's marketing department with additional ideas for how to best promote your book.

The promotional plan should be detailed, specific, and realistic. For instance:

- "I have six speaking engagements at large conferences scheduled for next year, where I will deliver keynote addresses to more than 50,000 attendees."

- "I will produce a book trailer that will appear on my Web site, which receives more than 15,000 unique visitors each day, and I will also publish the trailer on YouTube[SM]."

- "I will highlight the book on my weekly, nationally syndicated radio show with more than 80,000 listeners."

- "I will pre-sell the title though my monthly newsletter of more than 60,000 subscribers."

- "I will tweet excerpts from the book via Twitter[SM], where I have 96,000 followers."

Do not present vague statements, such as "I will promote the book on Oprah." Include concrete information: "I have received an invitation to appear on Oprah, once the book has been published."

About the author

The "about the author" section of the proposal presents your biographical information and expands upon your promotional ability. The purpose of this section is to:

- Establish your credibility as the best person to write the book.

- Demonstrate that your name or persona will help sell the book.

- Give the agent and publisher a sense of who you are as a person.

The "about the author" section may be written in either first or third person perspective. All the information you present should confirm your ability to write and sell the book. This section addresses the following areas:

Platform

A strong platform is essential to acquiring a book deal. This section may be the most important and most influential of the entire proposal. Present detailed, specific information to show that you have a strong, established platform that continues to grow. Mention your Web site, blogs; television and radio exposure; print interviews; published articles; the number of Facebook[SM] fans, Twitter[SM] followers, and LinkedIn[SM] connections; note how many subscribers you have for your newsletter or e-mail campaigns; highlight major speaking engagements; and if you have previously published a successful book, include the sales figures.

Credentials

You want to show the agent and publisher that you are a recognized expert on the topic you plan to write about. You can demonstrate this by highlighting your:

- Subject credentials: "I am the columnist for *Financial Times,* a respected financial journal read by investors and CEOs."

- Career credentials: "I have been the Vice President of Wealth Management Services for more than ten years, where I manage investments for Fortune 500 executives."

- Educational background: "I earned my Ph.D. in Finance from Harvard."

- Relevant awards or professional memberships: "I have be honored with the prestigious Golden Wealth Mentor award and serve as Director for the Professional League of Finance."

The chapter outline

The purpose of this section is to present a preview of the entire book. An agent wants to know that you will cover all the intended information, deliver the book's promise within the content, and package it in a form that is accessible to readers. The chapter outline presents the book's table of contents followed by a summary of each chapter.

Sample chapters

Sample chapters are excerpts from your book that highlight your writing ability and the style, tone, and depth of the manuscript. Each agent has different criteria for the number of sample chapters or pages he or she may request. Some agents may only ask for one chapter, others may want to see three chapters, and still others may request a specific number of pages. Plan to write the first two chapters, or at least the first 30 pages of your book, for possible submission.

Supplemental material

The supplemental material section, also referred to as the appendix, is optional. However, most agents advise including it when possible. This section contains additional items about you and your subject. Items you may consider submitting include:

- Published writing samples — may include magazine, newspaper, or online articles you have written related to your topic.

- Material about you — profiles and articles that have been written about you.

- Promotional material — such as business brochures, booklets, and conference publications.

- A color or black and white headshot — the headshot is a common inclusion in a book proposal and should be a professional 8- by 10-inch photograph, similar to an author's photo on a book. If you have a quality photograph of yourself participating in an activity that relates to the book, such as cooking, or surfing, or painting, you may choose to include it.

- Published material about your book's subject — photocopies of recent articles or features about the topic and its popularity.

- Summary of radio interviews and television appearances — if available, consider including a short, professionally produced clip on DVD.

- A selection from your portfolio — only if your portfolio is relevant and directly relates to your topic. For instance, if your book is about arranging flowers, you could include a selection of your best floral designs.

- A few sample images — charts, diagrams or illustrations that you plan to insert in the book.

FORMATTING AND PACKAGING YOUR BOOK PROPOSAL

The presentation of your book proposal is as important as the content. Print the proposal on white 24 pound, paper with black ink and 1-inch margins. Use a standard, easy-to-read font, such as Calibri, Times New Roman, or Arial, 12-point. All text is double-spaced, except your contact information, which is listed on the title page. Paragraphs are indented.

The title page

The title page is the first page of your proposal. Centered, one-third of the way down from the top of the page, is the title and author listing:

A Proposal for

Title of your book (printed in either all capital letters or italicized)

Subtitle or tagline of the book

by (your name)

In the lower left or right corner of the page, your contact informationis listed:

Your mailing address

Your telephone number

Your e-mail address

The proposal's table of contents

The first page after the title page is the proposal's table of contents. List each part of the proposal, flush left with the corresponding page number listed flush right.

The body of the proposal

Each page should be numbered consecutively. The page number is placed in the upper right corner. In the upper left corner of the page, include a header listing your last name and the title of the book (the title is printed in either all capital letters or italicized) divided by a slash: Author's last name/BOOK TITLE.

Supplemental material

All newspaper and magazine clips and additional material, such as brochures and booklets, should be presented on 8.5 by 11-inch paper. If necessary, photocopy the documents to conform to the correct size.

Packaging the proposal

Book proposals are usually presented in a sturdy, double-pocket folder. Do not staple the pages together. Place the complete proposal and sample chapters in one pocket and the supplemental material in the other pocket.

THE TOP TEN REASONS BOOK PROPOSALS ARE REJECTED

1. **The proposal does not contain a strong argument for why the topic is relevant, timely, and necessary.** How to fix the problem: Cite forecasts, statistics, and recent media attention surrounding the subject.

2. **There is nothing to differentiate this book from similar books on the topic.** How to fix the problem: Present a well-developed slant on the topic and clearly show how your book is different and why it is better than similar titles.

3. **The author's platform is not developed enough to indicate viable sales.** How to fix the problem: Establish and grow your platform with increased media exposure, ongoing publicity, and an extensive network of connections.

4. **The writing in the sample chapters is weak or not compelling or the author's writing style is overly academic.** How to fix the problem: Use active voice and include stories in your writing to engage the reader, enroll in writing workshops to become a better writer, or hire an editor or ghostwriter to polish the chapters.

5. **The author did not identify a specific, target market.** How to fix the problem: Carefully define your readers.

6. **The market is too small.** How to fix the problem: Include statistics and specialty marketing strategy suggestions.

7. **The author lacks credentials.** How to fix the problem: If you are not an expert on the topic, consider working with a co-author or obtaining the required credentials.

8. **The book will cost too much to produce.** How to fix the problem: Reduce the number of suggested images and lower the estimated page count.

9. **The author presented an article, not a book.** How to fix the problem: Widen your topic so it will qualify as a full manuscript and expand your chapter summary.

10. **The author outlined an unrealistic marketing plan.** How to fix the problem: Create a practical promotional plan with strong, specific strategies.

CASE STUDY: "HOW I ACQUIRED MY AGENT"

Alice J. Wisler
Web site: www.alicewisler.com
Blog: www.alicewisler.blogspot.com

Books: *Rain Song* (Bethany House Publishers, 2008), and *How Sweet It Is* (Bethany House Publishers, 2009)

Genre: Romance

Agent: Kristin Lindstrom, Lindstrom Literary Management

Ever since I was six, I wanted to write a novel and have it published. I started sending out query letters for a work-in-progress and waiting for agents to affirm me. Then the rejections came. After one particular rejection letter, which included personal feedback from a well-known agent, I realized that I had another problem besides the fact that I was querying for an unfinished novel: The main character's narrative voice was bland and she was not likable. I read a few pages from my novel again and realized I did not even like her.

I revised, and three months later I had twenty chapters I was proud of, so I sent out a query letter to an agent I found on www.agentquery.com. By nightfall, the agent asked to see my first three chapters. After she read them, she called to say she wanted the whole manuscript. Two weeks later I received another phone call. It was the agent — Kristin Lindstrom of Lindstrom Literary Management. "Alice, I love it, and I want to represent you." Within eight weeks, we had a two-book deal with Bethany House. *Rain Song* was published 20 months later and six months after that, *How Sweet It Is* was released. More recently, two more novels are under contract with the same publisher, thanks to Kristin.

Writing the Synopsis

A synopsis is a summary of your novel written in narrative form. There are two versions of the synopsis: the short-synopsis (two pages in length) and the long-synopsis (no more than eight pages in length). It is important to create both versions and have them available to submit to an agent, based on his or her requirements.

WHAT AN AGENT LOOKS FOR IN A SYNOPSIS

An agent will read the synopsis to determine if she should request the full manuscript. The synopsis is used as a guide to see if an author is capable of crafting a strong plot, creating compelling characters, and constructing a solid storyline. The main elements the agent considers when reading the synopsis include:

- **The author's writing ability.** Is the author a strong writer? Can he or she create fluid prose that leaps off the page and grabs the reader's attention?

- **The author's voice.** Does the author convey a clear, original, and distinctive voice that will draw readers?

- **If the writer understands his or her genre.** Does the author know the expectations of the genre she is writing in and can she deliver those elements in a satisfying and unique way?

- **The main conflict of the story.** Is the conflict interesting and compelling enough to engage readers?

- **The transformation of the main character.** Does the protagonist change and transform throughout the course of the story or does the hero remain flat and unaffected? What will entice a reader to follow the main character on his journey?

HOW TO WRITE AN EFFECTIVE SYNOPSIS

An effective fiction synopsis should deliver an entertaining reading experience and answer all the agent's questions.

- **Write in narrative format.** The synopsis is written in story form. It should not read like a chapter summary or outline, and does not contain any lists, bulleted points, or lengthy descriptions. A synopsis is always written in third person using present tense, regardless of how the manuscript is written.

- **Condense the story.** The synopsis includes only the main characters and major plot points. Leave out unnecessary and irrelevant details. Do not include subplots unless they have a major impact on the main storyline.

- **Succinctly summarize the plot.** There is not enough space to include every plot point in the synopsis. You should focus on the setup, the inciting incident, major turning points, the crisis moment, the resolution, and the obstacles and conflicts the main character faces, which test his or her commitment and ability to achieve her goal.

- **Tell the story in chronological order.** Regardless of how the story is presented in your manuscript, the synopsis should unfold in chronological order to ensure clarity and understanding, and to create an easy reading experience for the agent.

- **Include emotional turning points.** An impressive synopsis engages the reader by providing emotional impact and showing how the protagonist develops and transforms.

- **Express your voice and the tone of the story.** Your voice consists of your style — the form you choose to deliver the content. The synopsis should effectively capture your voice through the words and phrases you use, and convey the tone of your manuscript. If your story is comedic, the synopsis should be humorous. If you have written a thriller, the reader should experience the suspense of the story.

- **Create compelling sketches of the main characters.** It is often a story's characters that capture a reader's curiosity and interest. Presenting a captivating portrait of your main characters (including the protagonist, antagonist, and any key relationship characters) is an essential component of the synopsis. Devote most of your focus to your protagonist — show quirks, personality traits, wants and desires (internal and external goals), why it is desired, and what is at stake if failure occurs.

- **Do not introduce every character.** This is a condensed version of your story and it is not necessary to try to squeeze every character that appears in the book into the synopsis. For clarity and simplicity, try not to introduce more than four characters by name. When possible, use descriptive references instead, such as the butler, the dog sitter, or the neighbor.

- **Use dialogue sparingly.** In a synopsis, dialogue tends to distract rather than add to the effect of the story. It slows down the pace and can take the reader out of the experience you are trying to create. It is best to use dialogue only minimally — if at all.

- **Provide a conclusion.** In a synopsis you must reveal the ending. Never commit the ultimate mistake of telling the agent he or she must read the full manuscript to find out what happens. If you do, you will almost certainly receive a rejection letter. Be sure to present a conclusion, resolve all plot points, and explain why the main character made the decision that lead to the final outcome.

CASE STUDY: "HOW I WRITE A SYNOPSIS"

Kimberly Llewellyn
Web site: KimberlyLlewellyn.com
Blog: www.cleverdivas.com

Books: *The Quest for the Holy Veil* (Berkley/Penguin), *Tulle Little, Tulle Late* (Berkley/Penguin), *Tender Harvest* (Avalon/Thomas Bouregy), *Pretty Please* (Kensington Books), *Soft Shoulders* (Kensington Books)

Genre: Romantic comedy, Romance, Chick-lit, Paranormal romance, Non-fiction/YA

Agent: Zoe Shacham, Nancy Yost Literary Agency

The synopsis is a very important tool. It follows your book all along the submission process. Your synopsis will help an agent love your book. Your agent will use to entice and editor to consider your novel. The editor then takes it to her meetings to pitch to her peers to convince them to buy the book. Once bought, the marketing department uses it for promotion. They also use it to pitch to the sales team, which in turn pitches it to the bookseller, and in turn they hand sell your book to the reader.

I keep the synopsis as short as possible: five to eight pages. In fiction, the synopsis has to have a beginning, middle, and an end. I like to show the character arc, the growth of the protagonist, and the emotional journey. The synopsis needs to reflect the core of the story, the high points (plot points), and the climax.

Some of my synopses are offbeat or quirky in order to reflect my writing style, especially when writing funny chick-lit. Have your synopsis reflect the tone of your story. If it is a dark, gripping horror novel, let the dark language of the synopsis reflect that. Of course, if it is a romantic comedy, let your comedic voice shine through. If it is a sensual romance, use lush, rich words. It is all about your voice.

To avoid the sagging middle, I summarize that part of the book in a paragraph, writing something like, "Mary encounters more disasters, including a..." and then I list them. Or, "Further obstacles keep her from her goal, including..." It is fast and quick, and the agent can move on. Remember, you have to always give away the ending in the synopsis. Saying, "If you want to see how it ends, you will have to contact me" is a sign of an amateur writer.

FORMATTING THE SYNOPSIS

Present your synopsis using the following preferred standard format:

- Use 20-pound plain white paper and black ink.

- Margins are 1-inch all around.

- On the first page, place your contact information (mailing address, telephone number, and e-mail address) in the upper left corner, single-spaced.

- Immediately below your contact information, center the title of the book (printed in all capital letters), below the title type your name, and below your name type the word "Synopsis." Some agents also like the author to list the genre below the title of the book.

- On each subsequent page, include a header in the upper left corner with your last name, followed by a slash, then the title of the book (printed in all capital letters), followed by another slash and the word "Synopsis."

- Put the page number in the upper right corner on the same line as the header. Do not include a page number on the first page.

- The body of the synopsis is double-spaced with each new paragraph indented five spaces, justified left.

- The first time a character is mentioned in the synopsis, type the character's name in all capital letters.

When submitting a synopsis in the body of an e-mail

- Single-space the content

- Do not indent paragraphs

- Insert a line between each paragraph

- Do not include headers

- Do not include page numbers

- Place your contact information at the end of the synopsis

- Left justify the title and your name

CASE STUDY: "HOW I WRITE A SYNOPSIS"

Laura DiSilverio
Web site: www.lauradisilverio.com

Books: *Swift Justice* (St. Martin's Minotaur, 2010) and *Tressed to Kill* under the pen name Lila Dare (Berkley Prime Crime, 2010)

Genre: Mystery

Agent: Paige Wheeler, Folio Literary Management

When writing my synopsis, I use present tense, no matter what tense I use in the book. It reads better and sounds more immediate. I also try to infuse the tone of the novel into the synopsis. If it's a funny book, I use humor. If it is a tragedy, I use weightier language and dark images. I try to incorporate my narrator's voice into the synopsis so an agent or editor can get the feel of the book immediately. Voice is key.

Plot is equally important. An agent reads a synopsis wanting to know if the writer has put together a compelling plot, one that will sweep a reader along with the protagonist for hundreds of pages and come to a satisfying conclusion. A synopsis, whether it is one page or 12, should convince the agent you can deliver. I write mysteries, so I include as many plot points as necessary to show the inciting incident, the suspects and red herrings, how my protagonist follows the clues to the killer, and the conclusion. If you write sci-fi or fantasy, you need to show the agent you can create a world. Isolate what is unique about your genre and demonstrate that you have a handle on it in your synopsis. Show how your protagonist changes from the start of the book until the end. Sketch in the main relationships and character traits that make your protagonist human.

CASE STUDY: "HOW I ACQUIRED MY AGENT"

Lisa Lawmaster Hess
Web site: www.L2Hess.com
Blog: www.L2Hess.blogspot.com

Books: *Acting Assertively* and *Diverse Divorce*

Genre: Educational nonfiction, YA fiction, and Christian chick-lit

Agent: Diana Flegal, Hartline Literary Agency

I met my agent Diana at the Susquehanna Valley Writers' Conference. I had made an appointment for her to critique the opening pages of my manuscript. We just clicked. She was so friendly and upbeat and during the critique group, she offered all sorts of positive feedback. She had as much enthusiasm for my project as I did, so I knew she would represent it well.

The best advice I can give is to be honest about what you can and cannot do, but also be willing to take risks. Do your part — keep writing, build that platform, keep informed, and keep reading in your genre. Respect your agent as a person and as a professional, and remember that although your work is your baby, your agent is representing many other people's babies, too, so yours is not an only child. Do not allow bad feelings to fester — if you have frustrations then express them respectfully. Remember, too, that your agent wants to help you build a career, so keep writing.

Each agent has different preference regarding the length of a synopsis. It is easier to have them all on hand than to scramble to produce a new one when an agent requests one. I always send agents exactly what they ask for. I do not send five pages when they have asked for one page. When I have completed a manuscript, I draft a long synopsis around 15 pages in length and winnow it down until I have a ten-page version, a five-page version, a two-page version, and a one-page version. For the shorter versions, I eliminate many details, do not mention sub-plots, and summarize much of the story.

Preparing and Polishing the Manuscript

A the content of your fiction manuscript must be revised and polished until it sparkles, and then prepared, packaged, and presented following industry standard guidelines. Professional writers polish their manuscripts via:

- Story checklists or diagnostics

- Extensive editing and proofreading

- Using writing critique groups or beta readers

EDITING AND PROOFREADING

Editing and proofreading entails carefully checking your manuscript for typographical errors, spelling, spacing, punctuation, capitalization, sentence structure, syntax, word choice, tense, arrangement, and over-all clarity and flow. Techniques you may wish to use to proofread your manuscript include:

- Printing a copy of the manuscript and tracing each word with your finger so you do not overlook any errors.

- Reviewing your manuscript from back to front, so you are proofing the content rather than reading it.

- Reading the manuscript aloud to easily catch missing or misspelled words and lapses in clarity.

Professional freelance editors and proofreaders are available to assist you with editing and proofreading. The Editorial Freelancers Association (**www.the-efa.org**) provides a free directory of qualified editors and proofreaders and a standard rate chart. There are different levels of editing and types of editors to choose:

- A **proofreader** is someone who reviews the manuscript for spelling or grammatical errors. Proofreaders' fees average between $25 and $35 per hour.

- **Copyeditors** and **line-editors** read the text word for word and correct any grammatical mistakes or spelling errors. They also provide comments regarding content. The line editor will also make changes to the manuscript to improve readability, evaluate the text for consistency, and research and check the accuracy of facts. Basic copyediting costs $25 to $40 per hour and line-editors charge an average of $40 to $65 per hour.

- A **developmental editor** provides notes on story structure, character development, plot points, and dialogue. He or she may rewrite sections of the manuscript and rearrange content for better flow and logic. Developmental editors' fees range from $50 to $80 per hour.

WRITING CRITIQUE GROUPS AND BETA READERS

Writing critique groups and beta readers provide constructive feedback on your manuscript. They may offer different perspectives for you to re-evaluate your work and effectively revise the manuscript to make it market-ready.

Beta readers

Beta Readers are people who agree to read your manuscript and provide an opinion. Your beta readers should have an understanding and a passion for the genre you write. They may consist of your friends or associates. Virtual reader communities such as Library Thing (**www.librarything.com**) and Good Reads (**www.goodreads.com**) are excellent sources for finding beta readers.

Writing critique groups

Writing critique groups differ from beta readers in that they are comprised of authors with an understanding of the writing craft. The goal of a writer's group is to help everyone involved become a better writer, so each member participates in offering critiques of other members' manuscripts. You can find writing groups in your community by inquiring at your local library and independent bookstores. You can also locate writer's groups online by using a search engine or exploring writing forums. For Writers (**www.forwriters.com**) also offers a free listing of writer's groups around the country.

STORY CHECKLISTS

Story checklists are helpful for self-diagnosing problem areas of your manuscript. Many checklist books exist solely on this topic, such as Elizabeth Lyons' *Manuscript Makeover: Revision Techniques No Fiction Writer Can Afford To Ignore and Self-Editing for Fiction Writers* by Renni Browne and Dave King. Below is a story checklist to help you pinpoint weak areas and revise your manuscript for submission.

- Rewrite sentences that begin with the words "There" or "It."

- Revise sentences written in passive voice.

- Check that the tone is consistent for your story and genre.

- Ensure that all dialogue and speeches advance the story, and reveal plot and character.

- Make sure your prose is fluent and varied in rhythm.

Questions to ask when reviewing your manuscript:

- Does each of my characters have a distinctive voice?

- Is the antagonist as complex as the protagonist?

- Is the main character's opponent as strong or stronger?

- Do I open the story as late as possible?

- Does the opening grab the reader and compel him or her to continue reading?

- Is there enough conflict flowing through the entire book to hold a reader's attention?

- Is there a compelling reason for readers to connect with the hero and follow him on his journey?

- Does the plot unfold naturally?

- Have I crafted a key relationship for the protagonist that readers can relate to and root for?

- Is the theme consistent throughout the narrative?

- Does the writing evoke an emotional response for the reader?

- Do I have too much exposition delivered in one section?

- Does each chapter end with a cliffhanger?

- Does each scene contain conflict or tension?

- Have I successfully conveyed the main character's transformation?

- Are my descriptions vibrant and detailed?

- Does the ending pack a punch and leave the reader satisfied?

THE TOP FIVE REASONS A MANUSCRIPT IS REJECTED

1. The writing is too predictable — there are no surprises or twists.

2. The author does too much "telling" and not enough "showing" — stating how a character feels instead of showing it through action.

3. The characters are not interesting or worth caring about — there is nothing compelling to engage the reader.

4. The protagonist does not undergo a transformation — the main character is the same person at the end of the story as he or she was at the beginning of the story.

5. The author does not have a distinct voice — the style and diction of the narrative that is filtered through the author that creates a sense of uniqueness.

FORMATTING YOUR MANUSCRIPT

Proper formatting distinguishes you as a professional writer. Some agents and publishers may have their own formatting preferences. If you are unsure of a specific agent or editor's requirements, follow the common formatting and presentation guidelines outlined below.

- Print your manuscript on plain white 8.5 by 11-inch, 20-pound paper.

- Use a standard, easy-to-read, serif font such as Garamond, Times New Roman, or Calibri; 12-point.

- Text should be double-spaced.

- Indent each new paragraph five spaces.

- Do not justify the right margin.

- Each page should consist of approximately 250 words.

- Include page numbers in the top right corner each page, except the title page and table of contents page.

- Margins are 1-inch all around.

- Do not include any copyright information anywhere on the manuscript.

The title page

- Center the title, subtitle, and your name in the middle of the page. The title is typed in all capital letters and bolded. Below the title and subtitle, double-space and type "A Novel." Below "A Novel," double-space and type "by." Below "by," double-space and type your name.

BOOK TITLE

A Novel

by

Author's Name

- Type your contact information in the top left corner, single-spaced.

- Type an estimated word count in the top right corner.

Table of contents page

- Place a header in the top left corner with your last name, then a slash, followed by the title (typed in all capital letters), followed by another slash, and then the word "Contents." For example: Author's last name/BOOK TITLE/Contents.

- Center, approximately one-third of the way down the page, the words "Table of Contents."

- Four lines below "Table of Contents" list your chapters, each double-spaced in upper and lower case letters, flush left. Place the corresponding page numbers, flush right.

- Do not number the table of contents page.

- The margins of the table of contents page are 1.5-inches all around (all other page margins are 1-inch all around).

First page of each chapter

- Begin each chapter on a new page.

- Place a header in the top left corner with your last name, followed by a slash and then the title (typed in all capital letters.) For example: Author's last name/BOOK TITLE.

- Put the page number in the top right corner and on the same line as the header.

- One-third of the way down the page, bolded and in all capital letters, type the chapter number, followed by two hyphens and then the name of the chapter. For example, CHAPTER 3 - - ON THE ROAD.

- Four to six lines below the chapter title, begin the body of the chapter.

Subsequent pages of each chapter

- Place a header in the top left corner with your last name, followed by a slash and then the title (typed in all capital letters.) For example: Author's last name/BOOK TITLE.

- Put the page number in the top right corner and on the same line as the header.

- Begin each change of dialogue on a new line and indent five spaces.

Packaging your manuscript for submission

- To submit your manuscript to an agent via standard mail, place your unbound pages in a manuscript box (manuscript boxes are available from The Writer's Store **www.writersstore.com.**)

- Do not staple, paperclip, or bind the manuscript in any way.

- If you wish to receive a response from the agent, include an self-addressed, stamped envelope (SASE) in the box.

CASE STUDY: EXPERT ADVICE
FROM LITERARY AGENT
JESSICA FAUST

BookEnds, LLC
136 Long Hill Road, Gillette, NJ 07933
908-604-2652
www.bookends-inc.com
http://bookendslitagency.blogspot.com

Agency represents: Fiction — romance, erotica, mystery, suspense, women's fiction, and literary fiction. Nonfiction — current affairs, business, finance, health, women's issues, pop science, psychology, relationships, sex, parenting, pop culture, true crime, and general nonfiction.

On finding an agent: Do your research. There are many great Web sites to start you off with, including AAR and Absolute Write forums. From there I think it's imperative to get as much information from individual agent Web sites and blogs as possible. And then you need to follow guidelines, query, and be persistent. There is no secret to being published or finding an agent. It simply takes hard work.

On what she looks for in a fiction manuscript: A voice that resonates with me, strong characters, an exciting plot, a hook that differentiates your book from others, and of course marketability.

On what constitutes a good query letter: The best queries provide a real sense of the author's voice. A good query sounds like the book. If the book is a suspense novel, I feel the suspense in the query. If it's humor, I laugh by reading the query. A good query isn't boring.

On what she looks for in a book proposal: For nonfiction writers you must have a platform. The book proposal needs to show me that the author knows the subject, including how the book differs from others on the market, and it has to be interesting to me. Oh, and of course, I need to feel it's marketable.

On platform and credentials: Platform is imperative. Unless the book itself is so revolutionary that the book is the platform, I can't sell a book without a strong author platform — the media attention you get for the work you've done. This includes magazines, newspapers, radio, TV, and of course any workshops or speaking engagements you regularly do If a fiction writer happens to have a platform (a forensic psychologist writing about forensic psychology for example) that's great — however, it is not necessary. I am more interested in a fiction writer's credentials.

On trends: You should absolutely be aware of the trends. It always makes you a better businessperson to know what's going on in your business. That being said, you should never write to trends. Write what excites you and works for your voice.

On the synopsis: I look at how the plot unfolds (including the ending), how the characters develop, how the hook is incorporated, and I want to make sure the entire thing doesn't go off track if the chapters I read seemed good.

On the process of selling the book: Once a new client signs, and we both feel the work is ready to be submitted (it's rare anything is submitted without at least some revisions first), I encourage the author to start writing the next book while I work on enticing editors into big offers. I keep the author updated as much as possible and encourage communication if the author has any questions. As for time frame, there's no general anything in this business. I've sold books in 24 hours and I've had others take two years. Patience is definitely a virtue.

On maintaining a good working relationship: Communicate. An agent won't and can't do a good job if you aren't communicating your concerns, wants, needs, and desires.

CASE STUDY: "HOW I ACQUIRED MY AGENT"

Delilah Marvelle
Web site: www.DelilahMarvelle.com

Books: *Mistress of Pleasure and Lord of Pleasure*

Genre: Comedic historical romances

Agent: Donald Maass, Donald Maass Agency

Most publishers want manuscripts represented by agents. I knew I needed to acquire an agent to help me wade through the publishing waters without drowning. I had already developed a strong platform and credentials. I had published two books without an agent and I built my platform by basically branding myself; from my Web site to my blog, I have a brand that defines who I am as a writer.

I crafted my synopsis to unfold like a story and capture my voice and the tone of the book. I sent my manuscript to three readers and polished it based on their feedback. Then I began approaching agents. I contacted about 15 agents without luck. Then I met Donald Maass at a luncheon at Romance Writers of America's Writer's Conference. After the conference, I followed up with him and pitched my book. He requested the full manuscript within 24 hours and a week later we had a publishing deal.

What I learned is you have to trust your instinct and understand what you want out of your career before hiring any agent. It is not about getting "any" agent. It is about getting the right one for you. There are great agents who are perfect for some writers but not right for others. You need to keep the lines of communication open and give your agent the same courtesy you want to be given yourself.

SECTION 3:
Hiring a Literary Agent

Waiting for a Response

The amount of time you will need to wait for a response after submitting your pitch will differ for each agent. During this time you may receive rejection letters. Continue pitching to other agents, follow up with agents who fail to respond, and receive and respond to requests to submit additional material.

USE YOUR TIME WISELY

While waiting for a response to your query letter, book proposal, or manuscript submission, you want to continue to prepare for your career as an author. You can use this waiting period to:

- **Begin writing your next manuscript or formulating your next book idea.** Every author and literary agent interviewed for this book agreed that the number one thing every writer needs to do while waiting for a response is to write his or her next book (if you are a fiction writer) or outline his or her next book idea (if you are a nonfiction writer).

- **Continue to build your platform.** Increase your social networking activities, expand your blogging to include guest posts on other writers' sites, write author articles, submit your short stories to literary magazines, and make yourself available as a resource for reporters, journalists, and radio show hosts as a way to garner additional media exposure.

- **Prepare your next set of query letters.** When you have a stack of query letters prepared and waiting to be sent, any time you receive a rejection letter from one agent you will not have to waste time dwelling on the disappointment because you are ready to contact the next one — and increase your chances of becoming published.

- **Improve your writing skills.** The more you write, the better writer you become. The better writer you are, the more valuable, viable, and marketable your material will be. Devote more time to writing each day. There are many excellent books on the craft of writing that can help you, such as *The Elements of Story: Field Notes on Nonfiction Writing* by Francis Flaherty and *Fiction Writer's Workshop* by Josip Navakovich. Online and onsite writing classes, workshops, seminars, conferences, groups, and MFA programs can also improve your skills. You can find a listing of writer's colonies, MFA programs, and writing workshops in each issue of *The Writer* magazine, *Poets & Writers* magazine, and *Writer's Digest* magazine.

WHEN TO FOLLOW UP

Most agents' submission guidelines, available on their Web sites and in print listings, outline the agent's average response time for queries, books proposals, and manuscripts. This should give you a good idea of when to expect to hear from a particular agent. The average response time for:

- Query letters is two to four weeks

- Book proposals is four to six weeks

- Manuscripts is six to eight weeks

If you have not received a response from an agent within two to three weeks past the date of his or her listed response time, you should follow up with the agent. For follow-ups to book proposals or manuscript submissions, it is perfectly acceptable to call the agent and inquire if he or she has had time to review the material. For follow-ups to queries, you may send a brief note along with a copy of the original query letter.

Dear [Mr. Agent]:

I am following up on a query that I submitted to you eight weeks ago for my nonfiction book idea, MODERN TRADITIONS. As I have not received a response, I was not sure if my original letter landed on your desk or was lost somewhere in cyberspace. I am resubmitting my query, pasted below.

Thank you for your time and consideration. I hope to hear from you soon.

Sincerely,

[Author's name and contact information]

[Original query letter]

LEARNING FROM REJECTION

Rejection is an uncomfortable part of the submission process. Like all published authors, you will most likely receive many rejection letters. It is important, for your own peace of mind and for your professional success as an author, to maintain a positive attitude and persevere until you acquire an agent and land a book deal. Authors Jack Canfield and Mark Victor received 144 rejections before obtaining an agent and a publishing deal, and their book, *Chicken Soup for the Soul*, went on to become a *New York Times* bestseller.

Sometimes, rejection can be a gift. If the agent gives you notes, the advice can help you make constructive revisions and lead to a better manuscript or improved proposal. Most agents are too busy to have the time to write editorial notes. If you are lucky enough to receive feedback from an agent, be sure to send a thank-you by e-mail or postcard, and inquire if you may resubmit the work once you have made the suggested changes. Do not be discouraged if the agent will not accept the revised submission, simply move on and pitch the next agent on your list.

The more common type of rejection is a form rejection letter — a standard form the agent sends out when he or she chooses not to represent an author. Even though a form rejection letter does not provide specific advice to help guide your rewrite, it does provide a definite response, which releases you from waiting in limbo and allows you to continue pitching other agents — and move closer to your goal of becoming a published author.

TIPS FOR SUBMITTING ADDITIONAL REQUESTED MATERIAL

When an agent requests additional material such as a synopsis, sample pages, book proposal, or complete manuscript, it is important to remain as professional and responsive as when you sent the initial query.

1. **Send the requested material immediately.** Agents report they are perplexed when authors send material weeks or even months after it has been requested. If an agent is intrigued enough by your query to want to read your manuscript or learn more about your nonfiction project, send it immediately. Do not wait. If you do, you risk the agent losing interest, forgetting about you and your book, or deciding that you are unprofessional and not worth representing.

2. **Send the requested material via priority delivery service.** The purpose of using a priority delivery service is to ensure the material arrives in a timely manner to the right destination (on the agent's desk and not in the assistant's 'slush pile').

3. **Include a copy of the agent's request.** Often an intern or assistant will open the package. Inserting a copy of the agent's request for your material, along with a copy of the original query letter or a brief cover letter, indicates the material was solicited and ensures it will be delivered directly to the agent for review.

4. **Send only what is requested.** Be sure to send exactly what the agent has requested. Do not send the entire manuscript if he or she has only requested the first ten pages. Remember, following an agent's instructions demonstrates that you are a professional author who is easy to work with.

5. **Consider making requested revisions.** Sometimes after reviewing the additional requested material, an agent will respond with a request asking you to make specific changes to your manuscript or proposal and then to resubmit it. You will need to consider whether you wish to make the changes, if the revisions will benefit the material or project, and if you wish to continue to pursue possible representation from the agent. When an agent takes the time to comment on your material, it is usually because he or she feels there is good potential for selling the book and is seriously considering representing you. If you feel comfortable with the agent's requests then it may be in your best interest to make the revisions and resubmit the material for a second consideration.

CASE STUDY: EXPERT ADVICE FROM LITERARY AGENT

Rachelle Gardner
WordServe Literary Group
Web site: www.WordServeLiterary.com
Blog: http://cba-ramblings.blogspot.com
Twitter: @RachelleGardner
E-mail: rachelle@wordserveliterary.com

Books sold: **The Husband Project: 21 Days of Loving Your Man on Purpose and With a Plan** by Kathi Lipp (Harvest House, 2009) among many others.

On the types of authors and genres she is looking for: I'm looking for books that don't contradict a Christian worldview. In fiction, I'm concentrating on books that can be placed in the Christian marketplace, as well as general market fiction. Genres: Women's, Mystery, Suspense/Thriller, Police/Crime, Family Saga, Historical, Legal, Literary, Mainstream, Supernatural, and Romance. Pretty much everything except Fantasy or Sci-Fi.

In nonfiction, I'm looking at Christian-market and general-market projects: Home life, Marriage, Parenting, Family, Current Affairs, Crafts, Health & Diet, How-to, Humor, Memoirs, Money, Narrative Nonfiction, Popular Culture, Psychology, Science, Self-Help, and Women's Issues.

On what she looks for in a fiction manuscript: I look for a captivating, well told story. I'm looking for a unique hook that captures my attention, and a compelling voice that makes me want to keep reading. Most of all, I'm looking for writers who are ready for publication. This means, you have not simply sent me the first draft of the first book you've ever written, but rather you've studied the craft of writing, read books about it, taken classes or workshops, and honestly approached writing as the serious art, craft, and business that it is. You've taken the time to get objective feedback on your book or proposal, and revised and polished accordingly.

On what constitutes a good query letter: A good query pitches the book in a way that makes me want to read it, and also includes a small amount of relevant information about the author (which is more important for nonfiction authors than fiction). The point of a query is not to tell the whole story, but to make someone want to read the story.

On the importance of an author's platform: For nonfiction, the author platform is a very important consideration. You need to show that you have a built-in audience of potential book buyers, and that you have credibility in your topic. How to build a platform depends on what you are writing about, but anyone can begin to build a following through a blog and online social networking.

On being aware of publishing trends: Authors should write whatever they want, but base their publishing expectations on realistic evaluation of the market.

On crafting a nonfiction book proposal: The "competitive books" section is one of the most important parts. It's crucial to show the publisher that you know what else has already been written that's similar. It's also crucial to make your "author marketing" section as impressive as possible, without including any "wishes" or things you are willing to do. (Don't say, "Author is willing to promote, do book signings, radio interviews.") Only include things you will do and things you have the ability to make happen.

On what she looks for in a fiction synopsis: When I ask for a synopsis of a novel, I expect it to be one to three pages in length, and single-spaced. It should give broad strokes of the main plot, and the two to three main characters, being careful not to get too confusing with too many names or too many plot threads. The synopsis should tell the whole story, beginning to end.

On maintaining a good agent/author working relationship: It sounds cliché, but as with all relationships, communication is key. When you are confused about something, or disagree with something, it's crucial to discuss it with your agent. If you don't, misunderstandings can fester.

CASE STUDY: "HOW I ACQUIRED MY AGENT"

Laurie Pawlik-Kleinan
Web site: www.theadventurouswriter.com
Blogs: theadventurouswriter.com/blog-writing, theadventurouswriter.com/blog, theadventurouswriter.com/blogbaby, and www.seejanesoar.theadventurouswriter.com

Books: **See Jane Soar** (awaiting sale to a publisher)

Genre: Nonfiction, Health, Self-help, Inspirational

Agent: Jon Sternfeld, Irene Goodman Literary Agency

I approached a couple dozen publishing houses on my own, and found that it was too time consuming and energy draining. I would rather be writing and blogging than looking for a publisher, and I knew an agent could knock on the doors behind gates I could not get through.

I prepared an airtight book proposal with a strong hook and a well-thought-out idea, and polished it until it sparkled. I built a platform writing nonfiction articles for magazines such as **Reader's Digest, Health, Woman's Day,** and **More.** I am also the psychology feature writer for Suite101.com[SM], and I created and maintain four blogs. Then I crafted a catchy query to grab an agent's attention.

I researched agents. I looked at the **2009 Guide to Literary Agents**, explored Preditors & Editors (**www.anotherealm.com/prededitors**), and used a search engine to find "literary agents in America." I queried 14 of the "highly recommended" agents listed on Preditors & Editors and followed the submission guidelines. The agents' Web sites I visited had clear submission guidelines, and I took them seriously. The first agent I spoke to, told me he could not believe how unprepared and unprofessional writers can be. That made me realize how important it is to thoroughly edit my queries and proposals.

I was tempted to sign on with the first agent, but he suggested a fairly significant change to my book. He sent the contract and left the ultimate decision up to me. I decided not to work with this agent. It is important to interview your agent like you would interview an employee or colleague. Just because an agent offers to represent you does not mean you are a good fit.

Then Sternfeld contacted me to request my book proposal. Less than a week after I sent it we scheduled a telephone conversation. He was thrilled with my book proposal. "Even if you do not sign with me," he said, "do not change anything. It is great the way it is." We are now in the process of trying to sell it to a publisher.

Evaluating an Agent's Offer

When an agent is excited to represent you, he or she will often telephone you to make an offer or send you a personal note. Every writer knows that finding an agent can be a difficult process. Many authors become so desperate to acquire a literary agent that they simply sign a contract with the first agent who offers representation. Selecting an agent is a serious business decision and should be carefully considered. You want to ensure the agent is the best one for your book and the right match for your writing career.

QUESTIONS TO ASK
THE AGENT YOU MAY HIRE

Many of your potential questions about your prospective agent (such as the size of the agency, how many books she's sold in the past year, her specialties, the different publishers she has worked with, and how long she has been in business) will already be answered before you receive an offer of representation (you would have garnered this information from the research you conducted prior to approaching the agent). After you have received an offer of representation, other important questions will arise. The responses you receive will help you evaluate if you should sign a contract with the particular agent.

Schedule an appointment via telephone or in person to discuss your questions. The discussion should be a balanced exchange of information; you do not want to appear to be 'grilling' or 'interrogating' your prospective agent by reading from a long list of prepared questions. Let the exchange unfold naturally and choose to ask only a handful of the most important questions (based on your individual needs.) A list of questions you may wish to ask include:

- **Are you a member of the Association of Author's Representatives?** There are many excellent agents who are not members of the AAR, but lack of the required amount of sales and charging fees are two reasons an agent may be denied membership. If the agent is not a member, ask why and if he or she still adheres to their ethical guidelines.

- **How do you feel about my book and its potential?** The response you receive will help you gauge the agent's enthusiasm for the project. You need someone who will champion your book and not give up after receiving a few rejections.

- **Do you feel the manuscript or proposal needs edits before you begin pitching the book to publishers?** The response will give you an idea of the scope of edits he or she is expecting, and how long it will take to make the changes before the agent begins selling the project. It can also help you decide if you agree with the comments and are willing to make the requested revisions.

- **How do you plan to market my book?** The agent should be able to provide a clear strategy to sell your book. Will he or she pitch to several publishers at once or only one at a time? How many editors will he or she approach and what publishing houses will your manuscript be submitted to? If the agent cannot illustrate a plan, then he or she may be a disorganized and ineffective salesperson.

- **How often should I contact you?** It is best to have an understanding of expectations regarding communication before entering an agreement with the agent. If you hope to make contact once a week, and he or she implies that anything more than once per month is inappropriate, then the agent is probably not right for you.

- **How often should I expect to receive updates?** It is important to determine if you are a match regarding correspondence. Are you comfortable receiving an e-mail update once every two months or do you prefer contact by telephone at least twice per month?

- **Will you forward copies of rejection letters to me?** Obtaining copies of rejection letters from publishers is one of the few tools you can use to determine how productive your agent is in pitching your book. Some agents do not send rejection letters to their clients, but instead provide a monthly or quarterly summary of their marketing efforts. If you have a specific preference, be sure you select an agent who will deliver what you need.

- **How many authors do you currently represent?** If the agent represents a small number of clients, he or she will likely have plenty of time to focus on you and your book. However, do ask why he or she has so few clients. If the number of clients being represented is large (more than 50), ask how he or she manages so many authors. Does the agent have assistants and sub-agents? Find out how he or she plans to provide the attention necessary for your book to succeed.

- **How many of your current clients are published?** The percentage of authors for whom he or she has actually landed a book deal can provide insight into sales ability.

- **On average how many [insert genre] books do you sell a year?** If your prospective agent represents a variety of fiction genres, but has only sold romance novels and you write urban fantasy, it may indicate that — while he or she may be enthusiastic about urban fantasy fiction and want to represent you — the agent may lack the experience and connections to garner publishing deals for your genre. In such a case, if you decide to proceed with him or her as your agent, ensure he or she has a strong marketing strategy in place for your book — not simply an enthusiastic attitude.

- **What commissions do you charge?** The standard industry commission is 15 percent. You should not be charged a higher rate. If the agent offers a "reduced commission" plus a small "representation fee" — run fast in the other direction because such an "offer" is a scam.

- **Am I responsible for any other expenses?** Some legitimate agents may charge a nominal fee for photocopies, priority mailing costs, and faxing services. If an agent charges any other type of fee, it is an indication that the agent is not reputable.

- **What subsidiary rights have you sold for your clients and how is that handled?** You want an agent who is competent in selling different types of subsidiary rights, such as book clubs, film rights, foreign rights, audio, and serial rights. If your agent lacks this skill, you risk losing potential profits and exposure you would otherwise acquire with the sale of subsidiary rights. Some agencies have in-house departments that exclusively handle subsidiary rights. Some agents sub-contract other agents to handle the sales of these rights. For instance, your agent may work with a literary agent in Hollywood to handle selling film and television rights because the Hollywood agent has better connections in the entertainment industry. It is always to the author's benefit to have subsidiary rights retained by the agent. If your prospective agent informs you that he or she usually allows the publisher to retain the rights, you need to consider how such a policy will impact your long-term career.

- **What is your procedure and timeframe for payment of authors' royalties and advances received from the publisher?** All payments due to you from your publisher will be paid to your agent. Your agent deducts his or her commission and any additional agreed upon expenses from the publisher's check and then issues you the remaining balance. An ethical agent, who follows standard business practices, should have a non-interest bearing, 'holding' account for client monies that is entirely separate from the agency bank account. You want to deal with an efficient and organized agent who will issue your payment to you in a timely manner. The response to this question should indicate that he or she has good business practices and a well-managed system in place for sending authors' payments.

- **Do you issue an IRS 1099 form at the end of the year?** The Internal Revenue Service requires businesses to provide an annual 1099 form for each individual (who is not an employee) to whom the company has paid a certain amount of money. Your prospective agent should be set up to easily produce these forms each year. If not, it is an indication that the accounting practices are lax.

- **If you do not sell my book within a specific period of time, what happens?** Will the agent drop you as a client, allow you the option to find another agent, or continue to work with you to create another project to pitch?

- **How involved are you with guiding your clients' careers?** Your prospective agent's response will indicate his or her level of commitment to an author's career.

- **What happens when a publisher makes an offer; do you handle all the negotiations or do you consult with the author regarding the particulars?** Some authors prefer to be involved in every detail, while others are comfortable allowing their agents to control all the terms. Choose an agent whose method is right for you.

- **What happens if you go out of business, leave the agency, or pass away?** If it is a large agency, will another agent take over your representation, or will you have the option to hire an agent elsewhere? If the agent moves to another firm, will the agent transfer you to the new agency? If the agency closes, what will happen to your royalty statements and subsequent payments? You want to obtain a written agreement that outlines every possible form of exit.

- **Do you have an agent-author contract?** Some agents do not work with written agreements. It is unwise to hire an agent without a written contract. You are entering into a legal business partnership. A contract protects both parties by outlining goals, limits, and responsibilities.

AVOIDING SCAMS AND ASSURING CREDIBILITY

Unfortunately, unscrupulous people exist in any industry, and the literary world is no exception. Anyone can call themselves a literary agent, buy business cards, accept writer submissions, and take advantage of unsuspecting authors. When you have an understanding of how legitimate literary agents operate, you will be more able to protect yourself from predators. It pays to be knowledgeable and stay aware.

Here is a list of questionable agent practices to avoid:

- **Inappropriate fees.** Legitimate literary agents do not charge fees to read writers' manuscripts. Nor do they charge critiquing fees, retainers, or upfront office administrative or marketing fees.

- **Referrals to editing or book doctoring services.** A fake literary agent may tell you he or she likes your manuscript, but that it just needs some work, and for a fee he or she can edit it for you or refer you to a book doctor. In reality, this is a scam to collect your money without improving the work. If a "so-called" agent offers this service, move on to another agent.

- **No sales record.** Professional literary agents will discuss their recent sales with a prospective client. They should be able to tell you how many books they have sold, what types of books they sold, and to whom they were sold.

- **Refusing to answer questions.** A good agent will respectfully answer your inquiries and allow you to make the final decision concerning their offer of representation. Stay away from an "agent" who refuses to answer your questions, is rude or bullying, or pressures you in anyway.

- **Sending a generic acceptance form letter.** When a legitimate agent offers to represent a client, he or she takes the time to make a personal telephone call or send a note to the author. A professional agent would never remit a representation offer using a generic form letter containing wording that could apply to any book — only con artists do that.

- **Unprofessional contract terms.** Avoid agents with contracts that include perpetual agency clauses, claims on client's future commissions if the agency has no part in selling the property, billing clients for normal business expenses, provisions that ask for up-front payments, clauses for publishing through print-on-demand, or contracts that offer no advance.

- **Promises of publication.** A literary agent, regardless of how well established, can never guarantee he or she will sell your book. Unsavory "agents" use promises of publication to entice trusting writers.

- **Lack of contacts.** If an agent lacks publishing contacts that is a red warning flag. Obviously, established agents have extensive networks of contacts, but even new agents are not new to publishing and have lists of contacts. Using the resources listed in this chapter, research an agent's background and experience. Consider asking the agent to list a few editors he or she thinks may be interested in your work and why he selected those particular contacts. If he cannot answer that question, find another agent.

The Web sites Predators & Editors (**http://pred-ed.com**) and WriterBeware (**www.sfwa.org/for-authors/writer-beware**) each maintain a database of individual agents to avoid.

If you have been a victim of a scam or were misrepresented by an unscrupulous agent, consider contacting the following resources for assistance:

- The Federal Trade Commission, Bureau of Consumer Protection investigates fraud. You may file a complaint on their Web site at **www.ftc.gov.**

- Volunteer Lawyers for the Arts offers guidance and answers to your legal questions. Visit the Web site at **www.vlany.org**.

- The Better Business Bureau's Web site, **www.bbb.org**, allows you to search for information on a business as well as file a complaint.

- Contact your state's attorney general by visiting **www.attorney-general.gov.**

THE AUTHOR-AGENT AGREEMENT

Each agency has its own form of an author-agent agreement. You should understand and feel comfortable with the contract before you sign it. Ask the agent to clarify any terms or clauses you do not understand. You may also request reasonable changes. *An example of an author-agent agreement is included in Appendix X.*

The author-agent agreement may outline, note, or include the following:

- Confirmation that your agent is the exclusive sales representative for your work.

- The right of your agent to hire co-agents to help sell subsidiary rights.

- The agent's responsibilities.

- What work your agent will represent (usually all of an author's literary works in all forms).

- The duration of the agreement — some contracts have a specific period of time after which the author has the option to extend the contract or allow it to lapse.

- How notification must be submitted to terminate the contract. For instance, by certified letter with a 30-day notice.

- The agent's right to represent competitive books.

- The amount of the agent's commission.

- Additional expenses you are responsible for (such as messenger service costs, the purchase of review galleys, or attorney's fees).

- A clause stating that, upon request, you are entitled to receive an itemized list of expenses.

- The right of the agent to act as a conduit for payments received by the publisher.

- The remittance time for issuing payments to you after they are received from the publisher.

- You affirm that you have the right to allow the agent to sell the book. (In other words, you confirm that no one else can claim rights to the material).

- A clause stating that, in the event of your death, you have the right to assign the agreement to your heirs. This ensures that any outstanding royalties or income are paid to your estate.

- Which state's laws will be used to interpret the contract, should a dispute arise. Usually it is the state where the agent's office is located.

- The method that will be used to resolve disputes. For example, mediation, arbitration, or litigation.

- Both parties must approve a clause stating they agree to any changes to the agreement.

- Under what circumstances you can terminate the agreement. For example, this section may note what your responsibilities are if you leave before the contract expires.

- What your agent's rights and responsibilities are after the agreement ends. For instance, the agent may retain the right to sell subsidiary rights for any books he or she has sold while under contract.

How to protect yourself

If you are signing with a new agent who does not have an established reputation, you may wish to consider negotiating more specific terms designed to protect yourself should the agent be unable to sell your book or if you become unhappy with the relationship.

- **Include an exit clause.** This clause allows you to terminate the contract should anything go wrong. If an agent agrees to this clause, he or she will most likely include a stipulation that should your book sell in the future to any of the publishers he pitched, the agent is entitled to the commission. The agent may also require an extended termination notice, such as 120 to 180 days.

- **Limit the term.** If the agent does not agree to an exit clause, then insist upon a term limit that specifies a period of time (for instance, 18 months) after which if the agent has not sold the book, the author has the option to seek alternate representation.

- **Add a key man clause.** A key man clause specifies that, should your agent leave the agency for another firm, you have the right to terminate the agreement.

- **Request a cap on expenses.** If the agreement specifies that you are responsible for legitimate expenses incurred by the agency, ask for a cap to be placed on those expenses (for instance, $300 or $500).

- **Consider hiring an attorney.** If you choose to hire an attorney to review the agreement, it is important that the lawyer:

  1. Provide a fast turnaround time. You do not want to keep an agent waiting and risk having the offer rescinded, which is a common occurrence when lawyers become involved in the process.

  2. Is an expert in book publishing and agent agreements. Do not obtain the services of a general 'entertainment' attorney, you need someone who is adept in the publishing industry.

  3. Outlines his points to you, so you can approach the agent to request the changes. Never have the attorney contact the agent directly.

  4. Cleary defines his fee prior to reviewing the material. You do not want to have any surprises later.

CASE STUDY: "HOW I ACQUIRED MY AGENT"

Kristin O'Donnell Tubb
Web site: www.kristintubb.com
Blog: www.kristintubb.blogspot.com

Books: *Autumn Winifred Oliver Does Things Different* (Delacorte Press, 2009) and *Selling Hope* (Feiwel & Friends/Macmillan, 2010)

Genre: Children's, mostly middle grade and picture books

Agent: Josh Adams, Adams Literary

I had sold a novel previously without an agent and was a little overwhelmed and intimidated by the process. When the time came to submit my second novel, I knew I wanted an agent's assistance.

So, I ensured my manuscript was polished. My fantastic critique group slogged through many versions of *Selling Hope*, while I made revisions. I was also, without realizing it, establishing a platform and credentials through publishing one novel, and working on a number of work-for-hire children's activity books and magazine articles. I was also blogging and using social networking extensively.

I attended the Society of Children's Books Writers and Illustrators national conference where I met an editor with Feiwel & Friends/Macmillan. She critiqued the first few pages of the manuscript. At the same conference, I attended a session where Tracey Adams of Adams Literary spoke.

After the conference, I pitched Adams Literary. They requested additional material and I had a long telephone conversation with Tracy's husband and partner at the agency, Josh. I knew he was the right fit. I discovered that he and I had similar goals. Plus, his family and my family are similar, so I knew he would be able to relate to the fact that my full-time job is mommy, my part-time job is writing. It is wonderful to have a partner in this lonely business, but it must be the right partner. I feel very lucky in that regard.

When I signed with Adams Literary in February of 2009, I mentioned the editor I met at the SCBWI conference and the fact that she had expressed an interest in the story. They thought she would be a perfect fit, and within a month we had a book deal with Feiwel & Friends/Macmillan. It was all very serendipitous.

CHAPTER 12

Getting the Book Deal

A fter you have hired a literary agent, the next step in your writing career is to try to land a book deal. Your manuscript or book idea will go through many steps and stages before it is finally sold and published. You will also need to successfully navigate your relationship with your agent to keep it healthy and productive.

SELLING THE BOOK

Once both parties sign the agency agreement, the author-agent partnership is official and the process of selling your book to a publisher begins. The timeframe from when you first acquire an agent, to landing a book deal, to ultimately seeing your book in stores, can vary dramatically and is based on numerous components. Following, is a guideline of the steps involved with getting your book to the market and a general timeline to help you understand the process.

Step 1: The agent will work with you to make edits to the manuscript or proposal. Agents usually take on new projects they feel are strong enough to send out to publishers immediately. However, sometimes the agent will ask you to make edits and polish the manuscript or proposal further before pitching it to publishing house editors.

Your agent may provide you an editorial letter outlining the requested changes, insert comments directly on your manuscript or proposal, or — if the edits are minimal — simply discuss it with you in an informal telephone conversation. Depending on your agent's schedule, you may receive this within a few days or within several weeks. You and your agent will then determine a timeframe for when you will deliver the edits. Based on the scope of the changes, your material may go through several rounds of edits and may require a few days or several months to complete.

Step 2: The agent will pitch the project to a list of carefully selected publishers. Once the material is strong enough to send out, the agent will write a pitch letter (similar to a query letter) and approach several publishers he or she feels are good matches for your book. Most agents will pitch your project to more than one editor at the same time. Your agent may submit it to three editors or 40 editors simultaneously. Each individual agent has his or her own selling technique.

Do not expect your agent to share the list of the publishers he or she has approached, or is planning to pitch, until after the submission process is complete. An agent's job is to sell your book, and most agents prefer not to consult with authors about to whom they should be pitching (unless a specific publisher has expressed an interest). It is best to let your agent do his or her job and not interfere with the pitching process. The timing of the submission stage varies greatly depending on how widely the work is submitted and whether the material that is being read and considered is a 20-page proposal or a 500-page novel.

Step 3: When an offer is received, the agent will negotiate with the publisher on your behalf. It may take months or even years before you receive a publishing offer — or you may land a book deal the same day you hire your agent. There is no way to know how long it will take between the submission stage and the offer stage. Once a publisher does make a verbal offer, your agent will negotiate the major terms of the agreement with the editor. The negotiation process usually takes only a few hours to a few days to complete.

Step 4: The publisher will create a formal agreement. Once the terms have been negotiated, the publisher will construct a formal agreement. This may take two to 12 weeks.

Step 5: The agent may negotiate minor details of the agreement. Once the agent receives the formal publishing contract, she will review the details and may ask the publisher's legal department to make a few minor adjustments to the language contained in the agreement. This may add a few days to a few weeks to the timeline.

Step 6: The author and publisher sign the contract, after which an advance payment is issued. Once the final contract is agreed and signed by the author, the publisher will countersign it and issue your agent the initial portion (usually 50 percent) of the negotiated advance payment. Your agent will take the commission from the payment, and send you the remaining balance. This stage of the process may take four to six weeks.

Step 7: The author completes and delivers the manuscript. The average publishing contract gives the author six to 12 months to deliver the final manuscript. Most nonfiction authors will begin writing the manuscript as soon as they receive a verbal offer from the publisher. A fiction author's manuscript is already written when she or he receives an offer, however, the publisher may request a few changes, which will need to be completed before delivery of the book. Depending on the project, this stage of the process may take a few days or a year.

Step 8: Final edits are requested and delivered. Once you deliver the final manuscript, the editor will review the book and provide comments for final edits. The editor takes between two to ten weeks to provide the editing notes to you. Then you will make the final changes and resubmit it to the editor. Sometimes there will be several rounds of edits necessary.

Step 9: The book is put into production. Once the editor receives your final changes and the manuscript is 'approved,' the publisher will send the second half of the advance payment to your agent, who will then issue you the payment, minus the commission. Now your book goes into the pro-duction process, which consists of copyediting, proofreading, design, and printing. The publication date of your book may be six to 18 months after the manuscript is delivered and accepted (approved with final edits.)

Stages of the process	Timeframe
The agent requests edits to the manu-script or proposal prior to submission to publishers.	One day to three weeks
The author makes the requested changes and returns the material to the agent.	One week to six months
The agent pitches the book to editors and receives an offer.	A few hours to two years

The agent negotiates the terms of the verbal offer.	One to seven days
The publisher issues a formal contract.	Two to 12 weeks
The agent negotiates minor details of the agreement.	One to four weeks
The author signs the contract and the initial portion of the advance payment is issued.	Four to six weeks
The author delivers the completed manuscript to the publisher.	Two weeks to 12 months
The editor reviews the manuscript and requests edits.	Two to ten weeks
The author makes changes and resubmits the manuscript.	Two weeks to three months
The editor reviews the changes and approves the manuscript or requests additional edits.	Two to six weeks (Plus six to eight weeks if additional edits are requested)
The publisher issues the second half of the advance payment.	Four to six weeks
The book goes into production and is published.	Six to 18 months

THE PUBLISHING CONTRACT

Your agent will negotiate the terms for your publishing contract. Most agents deal with specific publishing houses so often, they already have a preset contract with the publisher that outlines agreed upon terms. Then all the agent needs to do is negotiate a few rights and terms particular to the author. The three most important areas the agent will negotiate on your behalf are:

1. The manuscript delivery and acceptance

2. The advance

3. Royalty payments

4. The subsidiary rights

Manuscript delivery and acceptance

The publishing contract will outline the date the manuscript must be delivered and stipulate that the publisher is only obligated to accept, pay for, and publish a manuscript that is satisfactory in form and content. Your agent will work with you to ensure the delivery date is practical and can be realistically met. He or she will also try to insert wording in the agreement that obligates the publisher to assist you in editing a specific number of drafts before the publisher can reject the manuscript.

The advance

An advance is the payment you receive prior to your book's publication. The advance is often based upon an estimate of your book's first-year sales. The amount is an advance against future earnings. An average advance for a first-time author is between $8,000 and $12,000. The advance is broken into two payments. One payment of 50 percent is issued at the time the contract is signed and the remaining payment is issued upon delivery and acceptance of the complete manuscript. Your agent will negotiate to get you the highest advance possible. Of course, the publisher wants to pay as small an advance as possible because he or she wants to ensure the entire amount paid to you upfront will be earned back through your royalties. Since you do not have to return any of your advance — unless the book is cancelled due to the author breaching the contract — the publisher loses the portion of the advanced amount that you do not earn back through sales of your book.

Royalty payments

Your agent will ensure you earn royalties for sales of your book that are appropriate with industry standards. Most authors receive a royalty of 10 percent of the book's retail price for the first 5,000 copies sold, a royalty of 12.5 percent of the book's retail price on the next 5,000 copies sold, and a royalty of 15 percent of the book's retail price on all copies sold after that. Your agent will make sure that the publisher provides a biannual accounting of your royalties.

Subsidiary rights

Subsidiary rights are all the rights (except for publishing rights) that are associated with your book that are available to sell. They include:

- **Reprint rights.** Reprint rights grant the right to print the book in paperback edition. In most current publishing agreements, the publisher retains the reprint rights.

- **Book club rights.** There are numerous book clubs that specialize in different genres and acquire book club rights to be able to offer your book to their members. Money, made from the sales of book club rights is split equally between the author and the publisher.

- **Serial rights.** A serial is an excerpt of your book that is reprinted in a magazine or in another book, such as an anthology or compilation. First serial rights allow excerpts to be printed prior to the book's publication. Second serial rights grant the right to publish the excerpts after the book has been released. It is more common for nonfiction material to be serialized than fiction.

- **Foreign language rights.** Your agent may use a co-agent in another country to capitalize on selling foreign language rights, which grant the right for your book to be printed in non-English speaking countries. Some publishing houses are already set up to publish in foreign countries. In this situation, your agent will allow the publisher to retain these rights, knowing the foreign house will print your book.

- **Electronic right.** Electronic rights grant the right to publish the book electronically. An e-book published on the Internet or a book purchased to read on an electronic device is a form of electronic publishing.

- **Audio rights.** Audio books often complement the printed version of the book. Audio rights refer to books that are published in audio form, such as on a cassette tape or compact disc, or delivered as a podcast available for downloading from the Internet.

- **Performance rights.** Performance rights allow your book to be made into a film, a television show, a video game, or a play or musical. An agent usually charges a 20 percent commission for the sales of performance rights.

- **Merchandising rights.** Merchandising rights allow the creation of products related to your book, such as calendars, greeting cards, games, or toys. The *Harry Potter* series of books by J.K. Rowling is an example of a franchise that produced numerous merchandising opportunities.

MAINTAINING A SUCCESSFUL WORKING RELATIONSHIP WITH YOUR AGENT

Agents hope to maintain positive, long-term relationships with the authors they represent. They are not looking to sell one writer's book and then move on to the next writer. An agent's goal is to create a successful partnership throughout a writer's career. Here are ways you can help sustain a healthy and prosperous relationship with your agent.

1. **Do not make unnecessary demands on your agent's time.** Your agent has many clients and responsibilities to tend to throughout the day. Be considerate and do not consume his or her time with unnecessary interruptions by calling every day, sending five e-mails an hour, or contacting him or her on the weekend to see if your manuscript has sold, yet. Contact your agent when you have a legitimate reason to do so, not just to 'check-in.'

2. **Understand the agent's role.** Once your book is sold to a publisher and the contract has been successfully negotiated, the primary job of the agent is done. An agent can feel frustrated if an author does not understand the agent's role, which can create problems in the author-agent relationship. Do not expect your agent to also be your editor, your confidante, your sounding board, your coach, or your publicist.

   The role of your agent is to:

   - Sell your book.

   - Negotiate the terms of your publishing contract.

   - Explain business issues and contract details when you have questions.

- Act as a buffer, should there be a dispute between you and your editor.

- Campaign on your behalf if your editor leaves the publishing house.

- Ensure you adhere to your publishing contract by delivering the manuscript on time and following the stipulations outlined under your option clause.

- Sell subsidiary rights (after your book is published).

- Strategize with you regarding the concept of your follow-up books and the overall vision for your career.

- Sell your subsequent books.

3. **Avoid micromanaging.** Recognize that your agent is a professional with years of experience and knowledge — the agent does not need you to telling him or her what to do. Respect your agent and let him or her do the job without interference.

4. **Never have someone else contact the agent on your behalf.** You are the agent's client —not your assistant, not your attorney, not your writing coach, not your spouse, not your publicist, and not your accountant. The agent expects to deal directly with you and will quickly become annoyed if forced to connect with other people on your team.

5. **Do not take your agent for granted.** Be appreciative of all the hard work your agent does on your behalf. Send a thank-you note when he or she gives you advice, lands you a writing assignment, or sells your book. Remember, she represents you because she believes in you and your work. Be sure to acknowledge the agent's efforts in your book's acknowledgments page.

6. **Share what you are doing to further your career.** Keep your agent updated. Send a short note whenever something good happens. For instance, when you receive a prestigious award, land an appearance on The Today Show, or send off the final edits to the publisher.

7. **Be faithful to your agent.** Your agent is committed to you, so be loyal to your agent.

8. **Retain a positive attitude.** It may take a long time to sell your book. You need to trust your agent and have patience. Remain dedicated to your career and determined to succeed.

9. **Deliver what you promise, on time.** If you are contracted to deliver an 80,000-word book, do not submit one that is only 35,000 words in length. If it is your responsibility to obtain special-use permissions before your book is submitted, ensure you acquire all of them. If you stated you would supply 15 images for use in the book, make sure you do so. If your publishing agreement stipulates that you deliver your completed manuscript within nine months, do not be late. Your contract is a legal document. You need to take it seriously because the publisher will. Do not agree to any terms that will be difficult for you to deliver. If you fail to deliver as promised, the publisher has the right to cancel your book. This reflects badly on the agent and hurts the relationship he or she has with the publisher and editor. The agent will not receive the remaining commission that he or she has earned and will be forced to return the commission already received. You will be forced to return the entire advance payment issued by the publisher, and will most likely no longer have an agent representing you.

10. **Work with your agent, not against.** Remember, your relationship with your agent is a partnership. You are both working

toward the same goal — to sell your book and establish your writing career. When your agent makes suggestions, offers advice, or recommends accepting a specific deal, work with him or her, not against. If you strongly disagree with the suggestions, advice, or recommendations, have a discussion with your agent regarding your opinion. Always keep the lines of communication open and respectful.

11. **Be wary of offering referrals.** Do not offer your agent's name indiscriminately to other writers who are seeking representation. Your referrals reflect on you. Only offer a referral to an author you respect and feel would be a good fit with your agent.

WHEN TO CONSIDER ENDING THE AUTHOR-AGENT PARTNERSHIP

If your book attains bestselling status, other agents will start contacting you. Prestigious agents from large firms may try to lure you away from your current agent. If your agent is doing a good job for you, think carefully before jumping ship for another agency. Remember, your agent believed in you and recognized your potential long before you achieved success — and helped you become a published author.

However, there may be circumstances under which the partnership with your agent is no longer working, and you may want to consider ending the relationship. Some of those legitimate reasons may be:

- **When there is poor communication.** If your agent does not stay in regular contact with you or does not return your calls or e-mails, he or she may be overwhelmed with too many clients and unable to devote the time needed to further your career. You have a right to receive a response from your agent in a timely manner. If communication has broken down, it may be time to seek alternate representation.

- **When an agent lacks integrity.** If he or she cannot explain efforts to sell your work, if you catch him or her in a lie, if you suspect participation in unethical practices, and you no longer trust your agent, it is time to move on.

- **When the agent is not productive.** If you do not agree with procedures, for instance: If the agent does not share the responses he or she receives from publishers, if he or she only pitches to one editor at a time and waits four months for a response, or has an assistant discuss progress reports with you, instead of doing it him or herself, then you must find an agent whose methodology is more conducive to your needs.

- **When the agent is not enthusiastic about your book.** You need an agent who is fired up and passionate about your work. You need someone who believes in your writing career and will diligently pitch your manuscript or book idea until it is sold. If your agent is not enthusiastic about your project, you need to find another agent who is.

Make a graceful exit

If you have done your best to attempt to resolve the issues with your agent — you have discussed it and tried to find a satisfactory remedy to the situation — and still the problems persist, you will need to formally end the business arrangement. It is best to exit the relationship with respect and professionalism. You do not want to become known as a difficult author who jumps from agent to agent. If your book has already been sold, your agent will still be entitled to receive earned commissions and represent the subsidiary rights, so you do not want to burn bridges. Move on with dignity and grace. Notify your agent of your decision by telephone (or in person, when possible) and then follow up with a certified letter confirming the new terms.

CASE STUDY: EXPERT ADVICE FROM LITERARY AGENT JOANNA STAMPFEL-VOLPE

Nancy Coffey Literary
& Media Representation
240 West 35th Street, Suite 500
New York, NY 10001

Joanna represents: Juvenile Literature (early reader to YA, nonfiction, and fiction); Romance (historical, paranormal, contemporary); Fantasy (urban fantasy and steampunk); Up-Market Fiction (women's fiction, dark fiction, literary, horror, and speculative fiction); and Narrative Nonfiction (environmental, foodie, and pop culture).

On how to find an agent: Research. I can't tell you how many writers I reject because they've queried me with something I'm not even looking for.

On what she looks for in a fiction manuscript: Strong voice, always. No matter how crazy or how dramatic the plot gets, a strong voice pulls me through.

On what makes query letter good: It has to follow industry standards: single page, 12-pt. font, 1-inch margins, contact info included, genre, and word count. It might seem obvious, but many authors don't follow these basic guidelines. After that, what constitutes a good query letter to me is one that tells me about the story.

On being aware of trends: Authors should always be aware of publishing trends because they should be reading — a lot — especially in the genre they write in. But that doesn't mean they should write for the trends. You should always write what you are passionate about. Always.

On "finding" authors: I do find authors. I read blogs, magazines, and anthologies all the time. I recently contacted a journalist I've been following. And since I represent children's books, I also read kid's magazines like Highlights and Cricket, so I'm always on the lookout for talent.

On the most common reasons a manuscript is rejected: The voice is weak, there is too much description, or there are info dumps of back-story in the beginning. All of those things are almost automatic rejections for me.

On how an author can learn from rejection: Even if the author receives a number of form rejections with no personal advice given, it's just another step in the process. There is rejection throughout this entire industry.

Writers get rejected from agents. Agents get rejections from editors. Editors can get rejections on a project from their peers, boss, or sales. Sales can get rejec- tions from book buyers. And then the reviews come out — the reading public can be harsh.

From every rejection along the way, it will hopefully make the author a little bit stronger and even more determined. Meanwhile, a writer should always be in the process of honing their craft whether it's working with a critique group, attending conferences, taking classes, or entering writing contests. No matter how many books you have published, there is always more to learn.

On what happens once a client is signed: Sometimes I take on clients whose manuscripts need a lot of work, but I just fell in love with the voice. And sometimes I sign someone whose manuscript is polished and ready for submission almost immediately. So the time frame drastically varies. I take a very active editorial role as long as the client is comfortable with that, so I will go back and forth with revisions, I get them second readers in-house, and I line edit when necessary. Once a manuscript is ready for submission, I write up my submission list. For every project it's different. I've done careful research and I choose editors who I truly think would be a good fit for the project and the author. It takes me a few days or more to write up my pitch letter, but when I first go out with it, it's over the phone. I like to show the editors how excited I am about the project and I like to gauge their initial reactions. Once I know which editors are reading the work, I e-mail the author the list of which houses are considering their work. Then, we wait. And wait. And sometimes wait some more. During that time, I'm actively following up with the editors and I'll even start working on the author's next project if there is something already to work on. As responses come back, I keep the author updated in a way that they feel comfortable. Some authors really want to know the minute a rejection comes in. Some want to wait until a few responses come in before I let them know. Either way, I'm always in communication with my clients about the process.

Tips for maintaining a good working relationship: Be patient. Agents have multiple clients and have to give attention to each one of them, and more importantly, agents have a job to do. I don't know of a single agent who just idles all day. We're in meetings, having lunch with editors, negotiating contracts, submitting projects, editing manuscripts, reading submissions, attending conferences, reading queries, and handling day-to-day issues and office work. Your agent wouldn't have signed you if they didn't believe in your writing — even if that first project isn't the one to sell — we simply just don't have time to take on things we're not 110 percent enthusiastic about. Your agent is one of your biggest champions in the industry, and he or she has your best interests in mind always (don't forget — your best interest is his or her best interest). Don't expect daily, weekly, or even monthly correspondence. I know you're anxious to get published, and if I'm your agent, I'm anxious for you to get published too. But I also want to make sure we start, and continue your career, in the strongest way possible.

CASE STUDY: "HOW I ACQUIRED MY AGENT"

Lisa Dale
Blog: www.LisaDaleBlog.com
Twitter: www.twitter.com/lisadalebooks

Books: *Simple Wishes* (Grand Central, 2009), and *It Happened One Night* (Grand Central, 2009)

Genre: Contemporary romance

I once interned at a literary agency. I would never in a million years want to go into a book deal without an agent. Having an agent is like having a partner to play good cop/bad cop with. You — the writer — are a nice, easy-to-work-with, talented artist. Your agent is there to act as the go-between when things go wrong — to protect the writer's reputation (among other things).

When I had completed my first contemporary romance, I got to thinking about who I had met who would most likely enjoy what I had written. A woman I had sat on a panel with at a conference many years earlier came to mind. Networking in person is a great way to meet the right people, regardless of where you are in your career.

I subscribed to Publishers Marketplace to research agents and I found her listing. She was a former editor, and her acquisitions and sales seemed to fit with my vision for my "brand" of books.

I wrote a query letter that demonstrated creativity and understanding of the business. Agents are business people — entrepreneurs, movers, and shakers. Most want to work with writers who are business people too. You have to be the total package: creative and practical. Having cred-credentials certainly helps, and your bio proves you have the talent and tenacity — and that, in turn, opens doors for you to meet people who will take you seriously.

I belonged to a writing organization (in my case Romance Writers of America). I knew joining the group was a way of showing that my interest in the genre was more than just lip service, and I knew they could point me in the right direction and teach me how the business worked. I had gone back to school and earned my Master's of Fine Arts in fiction. Going back to school afforded me the opportunity to earn a yearlong fellowship as the assistant editor of a well-known and reputable literary magazine. And eventually, my college nominated me for Best New American Voices. I also earned a Pushcart nomination. All these things look great on paper.

Though I am not the type of writer who participates in writing groups, I did run my manuscript by three close friends before sending it out to my agent. She asked me to revise the ending. The ending wasn't "wrong," but it just wasn't above average either. I did some more work, and when I brought it back to her she took it on. Books really are collaborative projects, and I am much indebted to my agent's patience and skill. We received our first offer for my novel *Simple Wishes* just two weeks after we sent it out.

Literary Agents
Looking for New Writers

Josh Adams
Adams Literary
7845 Colony Road C4, #215
Charlotte, NC 28226
info@adamsliterary.com
www.adamsliterary.com
Fiction: children's
Query: via mail

Emmanuelle Alspaugh
Judith Ehrlich Literary Management
880 Third Avenue, Eighth Floor
New York, NY 10022
ealspaugh@judithehrlich.com
Fiction: romance, women's fiction, historical fiction, urban fantasy, and paranormal
Nonfiction: narrative nonfiction, memoir, business, and how-to
Query: via e-mail

Bernadette Baker-Baughman
Baker's Mark Literary Agency
Post Office Bo x8382
Portland, OR 97207
info@bakersmark.com
www.bakersmark.com
Nonfiction: pop culture, sociology, narrative nonfiction, and memoir
Query: via e-mail

Matt Bialer
Sanford J. Greenburger Associates
55 Fifth Avenue
New York, NY 10003
Iribar@sjga.com
www.greenburger.com
Fiction: fantasy, sci-fi, thrillers, and mysteries
Query: via e-mail

Brandi Bowles
Howard Morhaim Literary
Agency, Inc.
30 Pierrepont Street
Brooklyn, NY 11201
bbowles@morhaimliterary.com
www.morhaimliterary.com

Fiction: sci-fi, women's fiction,
and literary fiction

Nonfiction: music, pop culture
science, humor, and how-to

Query: via e-mail

Laura Bradford
Bradford Literary Agency
5694 Mission Center Rd., Suite 347
San Diego, CA 92108
laura@bradfordlit.com
www.bradfordlit.com

Fiction: romance, erotic romance,
and urban fantasy

Query: via mail

Nathan Bransford
Curtis Brown, Ltd.
1750 Montgomery Street
San Francisco, CA 94111
nb@cbltd.com
www.curtisbrown.com

Fiction: literary fiction, YA, historical, and mystery

Nonfiction: narrative nonfiction,
business, sports, politics, and
pop culture

Query: via e-mail

Michelle Brower
Wendy Sherman Associates
450 Seventh Avenue, Suite 307
New York, NY 10123
submissions@wsherman.com
www.wsherman.com

Fiction: literary fiction, thrillers,
graphic novels, and YA

Nonfiction: memoir, pop culture,
humor, animal/pet books, popular
science, and narrative nonfiction

Query: via mail

Sheree Bykofsky
Sheree Bykofsky Associates, Inc.
4326 Harbor Beach Blvd.
Post Office Box 706
Brigatine, NJ 08203
submitbee@aol.com
www.shereebee.com

Fiction: literary fiction
and mysteries

Nonfiction: business, parenting,
relationships, personal finance,
self-help, biography, current affairs, women's issues, cookbooks,
spiritual, and how-to

Query: via e-mail

Danielle Chiotti
Upstart Crow Literary
Post Office Box 25404
Brooklyn, NY 11202
Danielle@upstartcrow.com
www.upstartcrowliterary.com

Fiction: women's fiction, multicultural fiction, romance, paranormal romance, and YA

Nonfiction: narrative nonfiction, memoir, self-help, relationships, humor, current events, women's issues and cooking

Query: via e-mail

Vivian Chum
Prospect Agency
285 Fifth Avenue, Mail Box 445
Brooklyn, NY 11215
www.prospectagency.com
Fiction: YA, MG, romance, women's fiction, and literary fiction

Nonfiction: historical, pop culture, legal, political, and edgy memoir

Query: via Web site submission form

Greg Daniel
Daniel Literary Group
1701 Kingsbury Drive, Suite 100
Nashville, TN 37215
submissions@danielliterarygroup.com
www.danielliterarygroup.com
Fiction: religious, and true crime

Nonfiction: any category (especially if author is an expert with a platform)

Query: via e-mail

Lucienne Diver
The Knight Agency
submissions@knightagency.net
www.knightagency.net
Fiction: fantasy, sci-fi, romance, mystery, suspense, erotica, and YA

Query: via e-mail

Scott Egan
Greyhaus Literary Agency
3021 20th Street PL SW
Puyallup, WA 98373
www.greyhausagency.com
Fiction: women's lit, romance, paranormal, and romance suspense

Query: via mail

Susanna Einstein
LJK Literary Management, LLC
708 3rd Avenue, 16th Floor
New York, NY 10017
submissions@ljkliterary.com
www.ljkliterary.com
Fiction: literary fiction, YA, crime, historical, and women's fiction

Query: via e-mail or mail

Caren Estesen
Johnson Literary
132 East 43rd Street, Suite 216
New York, NY 10017
johnsonlitagency@gmail.com
www.johnsonliterary.com
Fiction: romance, romantic suspense, contemporary romance,

historical romance, women's fiction, thriller, and YA

Nonfiction: social sciences, women's issues, and history

Amberly Finarelli
Andrea Hurst Literary Management
Post Office Box 19010
Sacramento, CA 95819
amberly@andreahurst.com
www.andreahurst.com

Fiction: women's fiction, comic mystery, cozy mystery, and literary fiction

Nonfiction: humor/gift books, crafts, how-to (financial, house and home, health and beauty, weddings), relationships/advice, self-help, psychology, travel writing, and narrative nonfiction
Query: via mail

Diana Flegal
Hartline Literary
123 Queenston Drive
Pittsburgh, PA 15235
Diana@hartlineliterary.com
www.hartlineliterary.com

Fiction: contemporary fiction (not in conflict with a Christian world view)

Nonfiction: how-to, parenting, marriage, arts, and health (not in conflict with a Christian world view)

Query: via e-mail

Emily Forland
The Wendy Weil Agency
232 Madison Avenue, Suite 130
New York, NY 10016
www.wendyweil.com

Fiction: literary fiction, and mystery/thriller

Nonfiction: memoir, narrative nonfiction, journalism, history, current affairs, health, science, pop culture, lifestyle, and art history
Query: via mail

Diane Freed
FinePrint Literary Management
240 West 35th, Suite 500
New York, NY 10001
diane@fineprintlit.com
www.fineprintlit.com

Fiction: literary fiction, and women's fiction

Nonfiction: advice, relationships, spirituality, inspiration, health, fitness, memoir, narrative nonfiction, pop culture, lifestyle, women's issues, the environment, and humor
Query: via e-mail

Lilly Ghahremani
Full Circle Literary
submissions@fullcircleliterary.com
www.fullcircleliterary.com

Fiction: women's fiction, literary fiction, and multicultural

Nonfiction: pop culture, parenting, crafts, green living, how-to, business, and multicultural

Query: via e-mail

Mollie Glick
Foundry Literary and Media
33 West 17th Street
Penthouse, New York NY 10011
www.foundrymedia.com
Fiction: literary fiction
Nonfiction: popular science, medical, psychology, cultural history, memoir, and current events
Query: via mail

Loren S. Grossman
Paul S. Levine Literary Agency, Inc.
1054 Superba Avenue
Venice, CA 90291
lrg@ix.netcom.com
www.paulslevinelit.com
Nonfiction: child guidance, parenting, education, academics, health, science, and technology
Query: via e-mail

Sammie L. Justesen
Northern Lights Literary Services
11248 N. Boyer Road, Suite A
Sandpoint, ID 83864
Sammie@northerlightsls.com
www.northernlightsls.com
Fiction: women's fiction, romance, mystery, Christian, and suspense

Nonfiction: health, biography, psychology, self-help, how-to, food, parenting, new age, medical, and business

Query: via e-mail

Abigail Koons
The Park Literary Group
270 Lafayette Street, Suite 1504
New York, NY 10012
queries@parkliterary.com
www.parkliterary.com
Fiction: thriller and mystery
Nonfiction: popular science, history, politics, current events, adventure travel, and travel narrative
Query: via e-mail

Jennifer Laughran
Andrea Brown Literary Agency, Inc.
1076 Eagle Drive
Salinas, CA 93905
jennl@andreabrownlit.com
www.andreabrownlit.com
Fiction: children's, and YA.
Query: via e-mail

Kristin Lindstrom
Lindstrom Literary
Management, LLC
871 North Greenbriar Street
Arlington, VA 22205
kristin@lindstromliterary.com
www.lindstromliterary.com

Fiction: action/adventure, detective, erotica, mystery/suspense, religious/inspirational, thriller, and women's fiction

Nonfiction: animals, biography, business, current affairs, history, memoir, pop culture, science/technology, and true crime

Query: via mail

Alexandra H. Machinist
The Linda Chester and Associates
Literary Agency
630 Fifth Avenue, Suite 2036
Rockefeller Center
New York, NY 10111
alexandra@lindachester.com
www.lindachester.com

Fiction: literary fiction, upmarket women's fiction, historical, historical romance, and paranormal romance

Nonfiction: narrative nonfiction, pop culture, popular science, and travel narrative

Query: via e-mail

Jennifer Mattson
Andrea Brown Literary Agency
1076 Eagle Drive
Salinas, CA 93905
jmatt@andreabrownlit.com
www.andreabrownlit.com

Fiction: fantasy, alternate realities, magical realism, and steampunk

Query: via e-mail

Jeffrey McGraw
The August Agency
submissions@augustagency.com
www.augustagency.com

Fiction: women's fiction

Nonfiction: political sciences, history, biography, self-help, health, lifestyle, and social sciences

Query: via e-mail

Kate McKean
Howard Morhaim
Literary Agency
30 Pierrepont Street
Brooklyn, NY 11201
kmckean@morhaimliterary.com
www.morhaimliterary.com

Fiction: literary fiction, contemporary women's fiction, paranormal romance, romantic suspense, urban fantasy, mystery, and YA and MG fiction

Nonfiction: narrative nonfiction, sports-related books, food writing, pop culture, and crafts

Query: via e-mail

Laurie McLean
Larsen Pomada Literary Agents
Post Office Box 258
La Honda, CA 94020
laurie@agentsavant.com
www.agentsavant.com

Fiction: romance, fantasy, horror, mysteries, new Westerns, suspense, thrillers, children's, and YA

Query: via e-mail

Courtney Miller-Callihan
Sanford J. Greenburger Associates
55 Fifth Avenue, 15th Floor
New York, NY 10003
cmiller@sjga.com
www.greenburger.com
Fiction: historical, commercial
women's fiction, and children's
Nonfiction: practical/how-to
books, self-help, pop culture, lifestyle, and narrative nonfiction
Query: via e-mail

Robin Mizell
Robin Mizell Ltd.
Post Office Box 1270
Athens, OH 45701
mail@robinmizell.com
www.robinmizell.com
Fiction: literary and commercial
fiction, graphic novels, YA, and
short-story collections
Nonfiction: narrative journalism,
neuroscience, psychology, sociology, pop culture, memoir,
and biography
Query: via e-mail

Tamela Hancock Murray
Hartline Literary
10383 Godwin Drive
Manassas, VA 20110

tamela@hartlineliterary.com
www.hartlineliterary.com
Fiction: Christian romance, and
historical Christian
Query: via e-mail

Joe Monti
Barry Goldblatt Literary, LLC
320 7th Avenue, Suite 266
Brooklyn, NY 11215
query@bgliterary.com
www.bgliterary.com
Fiction: graphic novels, fantasy,
sci-fi, children's and YA
Query: via e-mail

Ellen Pepus
Signature Literary Agency
ellen@signaturelit.com
www.signaturelit.com
Fiction: literary fiction, women's
fiction, romance, historical,
erotica, and mysteries
Nonfiction: narrative nonfiction,
memoir, food, travel, pop culture,
and self-help
Query: via e-mail

Alanna Rammirez
Trident Media Group
41 Madison Avenue, Floor 36
New York, NY 10010
www.tridentmediagroup.com
Fiction: literary fiction

Nonfiction: narrative nonfiction, memoir, and lifestyle

Query: via mail

Victoria Sanders
Victoria Sanders & Associates
241 Avenue of the America,
Suite 11 H
New York, NY 10014
queriesvsa@hotmail.com
www.victoriasanders.com

Fiction: action/adventure, family saga, feminist, gay/lesbian, literary fiction, and thrillers

Nonfiction: biography, current affairs, gay/lesbian, political, legal, pop culture, and psychology.

Query: via e-mail

Katherine Sands
Sarah Jane Freymann Literary
Agency
200 East 62nd Street, Suite 30D
New York, NY 10065
sarah@sarahjanefreymann.com
www.sarahjanefreymann.com

Fiction: literary fiction, chick-lit, and commercial fiction

Nonfiction: food, travel, lifestyle, home arts, beauty, wisdom, relationships, parenting, pop culture, and memoir

Query: via e-mail

Jessica Sinsheimer
Sarah Jane Freymann
Literary Agency
59 West 71st Street, Suite 9B
New York, NY 10023
submissions@sarahjanefreymann.com
www.sarahjanefreymann.com

Fiction: literary fiction, YA, and women's fiction

Nonfiction: food memoir, travel memoir, parenting, psychology, and cookbooks

Query: via e-mail

Gretchen Stelter
Baker's Mark Literary Agency
Post Office Box 8382
Portland, OR 97207
info@bakersmark.com
www.bakersmark.com

Fiction: MG and YA

Query: via e-mail

Jon Sternfeld
Irene Goodman Literary Agency
27 West 24th Steet, Suite 700B
New York, NY 10010
queries@irenegoodman.com
www.irenegoodman.com

Fiction: literary fiction

Nonfiction: narrative nonfiction

Query: via e-mail

Elisabeth Weed
Weed Literary, LLC

27 West 20th Street
New York, NY 10011
www.weedliterary.com

Fiction: upmarket women's fiction

Nonfiction: narrative nonfiction, investigative, and women's issues

Query: via mail

Ted Weinstein
Ted Weinstein Literary Management
submissions@twliterary.com
www.twliterary.com

Nonfiction: biography, business, current events, politics, health, history, political, science, self-help, personal improvement, travel, and narrative journalism

Query: via e-mail

Jennifer Weltz
Jean V. Neggar Literary Agency
216 East 75th Street, Suite 1E
New York, NY 10021
jweltz@jvnla.com
www.jvnla.com

Fiction: women's fiction, thrillers, historical, and romance

Query: via e-mail

Natanya Wheeler
Nancy Yost Literary
350 Seventh Avenue, Suite 2003
New York, NY 10001
querynatanya@nyliterary.com
www.nyliterary.com

Fiction: literary fiction, family sagas, edgy thrillers, and cozy mysteries

Nonfiction: nature, women's issues, alternative lifestyles, green living, and food

Query: via e-mail

Paige Wheeler
Folio Literary Management, LLC
505 Eighth Avenue, Suite 603
New York, NY 10018
www.foliolit.com

Fiction: erotica, fantasy, mystery/suspense, romance, thriller, and edgy crime

Nonfiction: business, parenting, history, how-to, memoir, military, pop culture, self-help, narrative nonfiction, biography, crime, and cookbooks

Query: via mail

Christine Witthohn
Book Cents Literary Agency
2011 Quarrier Street
Charlston, WV 25311
cs@bookcentsliteraryagency.com
www.bookcentsliteraryagency.com

Fiction: contemporary romance, romantic comedies, paranormal romance, mystery/suspense romance, chick-lit, mystery/suspense, literary fiction, and YA

Nonfiction: women's issues, gardening, travel, outdoor adventure, and cookbooks

Query: via e-mail

** *These listings were accurate and up to date at press time. However, agents often change agencies or redefine what they are seeking. Be sure to visit each agent's Web site for current guidelines prior to submitting a query.*

National Writer's Organizations

American Christian Writers
www.acwriters.com

American Christian
Fiction Writers
www.acfw.com

American Crime Writers League
www.acwl.org

The Author's Guild
www.authorsguild.org

Chick Lit Writers
www.chicklitwriters.com

Historical Novel Society
www.historicalnovelsociety.org

Horror Writers Association
www.horror.org

International Association of
Crime Writers
www.crimewritersna.org

International Autobiography /
Biography Association
www.iaba.org.cn

International Food, Wine, and
Travel Writers Association
www.ifwtwa.org

International Thriller
Writers Association
www.thrillerwriters.org

Mystery Writers of America
www.mysterywriters.org

*National Association of
Memoir Writers*
www.namw.org

*National Association of
Women Writers*
www.naww.org

National Writers Association
www.nationalwriters.com

Romance Writers of America
www.rwanational.org

*Science Fiction and Fantasy
Writers of America*
www.sfwa.org

Sisters in Crime
www.sistersincrime.org

*Society of Children's Book
Writers and Illustrators*
www.scbwi.org

Western Writers of America, Inc.
www.westernwriters.org

National Writer's Conferences

Agents and Editors Conference
www.writersleague.org
Annual conference held each summer. Offers writers to the opportunity to meet with agents and editors.

ASJA Writers Conference
www.asjaconference.org
Annual conference held in April. Offers sessions of nonfiction writing.

Book Expo America
www.writersdigest.com/bea
Annual conference held in May. Offers instruction on writing and advice for submitting work.

East of Eden Writers Conference
www.southbaywriters.com
Biannual conference held in September. Pitch sessions to agents and publishers are available.

Glorieta Christian Writers Conference
www.glorietacwc.com
Annual conference held in October for agents, editors, and writers of Christian books.

La Jolla Writers Conference
www.lajollawritersconference.com
Annual conference held in October. Agents, publishers, editors, and publicists teach classes.

Magna Cum Murder
www.magnacummurder.com
Annual conference held in October for crime writers.

Maui Writers Conference
www.mauiwriters.com
Annual conference held Labor Day weekend. Sessions with agents and publishers, and one-on-one consultations available.

North Carolina Writer's Network Fall Conference
www.ncwriters.org

Annual conference held in November. Agents teach seminars and are available for pitch sessions.

Pikes Peak Writers Conference
www.ppwc.net

Annual conference held in April. Focus is on writing and publishing genre fiction.

Pima Writers' Workshops
www.pima.edu

Annual conference held in May. Agents are available for meetings with attendees.

PNWA Summer Writers Conference
www.pnwa.org

Annual conference held in July. Attendees have the opportunity to meet with agents and editors.

San Francisco Writers Conference
www.sfwriters.org

Annual conference held President's Day weekend. Top authors and respected literary agents are in attendance.

Santa Barbara Writers Conference
www.sbwritersconference.com

Annual conference held in June. Speakers include authors, publishers, and agents.

Society of Children's Book Writers & Illustrators Conference
www.hofstra.edu/ucce/childlitconf

Annual conference held in August. Brings together agents, publishers, writers, and illustrators of children's books.

Willamette Writers Conference
www.willamettewriters.com

Annual conference held in August. Agents speak on the publishing industry and are available for meetings with attendees.

Writer's Digest Conference
www.writersdigestconference.com

Annual conference held in September. Sessions with agents, authors, and editors on the business of getting published.

Genre Definitions

Action Thriller: A story that incorporates a ticking-clock scenario and violent battle scenes.

Alternate History: A novel that speculates on historical events.

Amateur Detective: A mystery story solved by someone who is not a detective.

Arthurian Fantasy: A story that features the legend of King Arthur and the Knights of the Round Table.

Autobiography: An account of a person's life written by the subject himself.

Bangsian Fantasy: A novel that speculates on the afterlives of famous people.

Biopunk: A story that blends noir, Japanese anime, and postmodern elements to create an underground, nihilistic biotech society.

Chick-Lit: Humorous romantic adventures designed for female readers in their 20s and 30s.

Child in Peril: Mystery or horror stories that involve the abduction or abuse of a child.

Children's Fantasy: A fantasy story written specifically for young readers.

Christian Romance: Romances in which both the hero and heroine are Christians who adhere to Christian ideals.

Classic Whodunit: A story in which a detective solves the crime, with the author presenting numerous clues for the reader.

Comic Horror: Novels that spoof horror conventions or present the horror with elements of dark humor.

Comic Mystery/Bumbling Detective: A mystery story featuring humor in which the detective is incompetent, but somehow manages to solve the crime anyway.

Comic Sci-Fi/Fantasy: A story the either spoofs the fantasy or science fiction genre or incorporates humorous elements.

Comic Thriller: Either includes comedic elements or spoofs the thriller/suspense genre.

Commercial Fiction: Novels that appeal to a wide audience.

Conspiracy: A thriller in which the hero or heroine uncovers a conspiracy by a large, powerful group.

Contemporary Romance: A romance with modern characters and true-to-life settings.

Courtroom Drama: A mystery tale that centers on the justice system; usually the hero is a defense attorney who must prove his client's innocence.

Cozy: A mystery tale that takes place in a small town or home where all the suspects are present and familiar with one another, except the detective who is usually an outsider.

Creepy Kids: A horror story in which children are controlled by dark forces and turn against adults.

Crime Thriller: A tale that focuses on the commission of a crime, often from the point of view of the perpetrators.

Cyberpunk: Sci-fi stories that feature tough outsiders in a high-tech, dehumanized future setting.

Dark Fantasy: Fantasy tales that focus on the darker side of magic, incorporating violence and elements of horror or a horror story that incorporates supernatural and fantasy elements.

Dark Mystery/Noir: Hardboiled detective stories presented in an urban setting with morally ambiguous characters.

Disaster: A story that presents natural elements as the antagonist, such as an earthquake or hurricane.

Dystopian: Fantasy or sci-fi stories that present a bleak future world.

Eco-Thriller: A story in which the hero must battle an ecological catastrophe and the people who created it.

Erotica or Romantica: A romance story that depicts explicit sexual scenes.

Erotic Fantasy: Fantasy tales that focus on sexuality.

Erotic Thriller: A suspense in which sexual aspects are a major part of the story.

Erotic Vampire: Emphasizes the sexuality in a vampire story and includes graphic violence.

Espionage: A thriller/suspense in which the hero is an international spy.

Espionage Mystery: A story that incorporates elements of the international spy novel, but focuses more on the puzzle that must be solved.

Fabulist: A horror tale where objects, animals, or forces are given human characteristics to deliver a moral message.

Fantasy: Fiction that features elements of magic, wizardry, and the supernatural.

Forensic: A thriller or mystery story that features forensic experts and focuses on forensic labs and detailed scientific procedures.

Game-Related Fantasy: These are stories based on a specific role-playing game, such as Dungeons and Dragons.

Glitz/Glamour: A romance story that follows elite celebrity-like characters as they live a glamorous life traveling around the world.

Gothic: A story that combines elements of horror and romance with medieval props, such as castles, darkness, and decay.

Hard Science Fiction: Tales set in the future that incorporate real-life, current-day science.

Hauntings: A horror tale that focuses on a structure that is possessed by a ghost, demon, or poltergeist.

Heists and Capers: A crime tale that focuses on the planning and execution of a crime, told from the criminal's perspective.

Heroic Fantasy: A tale that focuses on the heroes of fantastical wars.

High/Epic Fantasy: Stories that feature a young hero battling an evil entity to save the fate of an entire race or nation.

Historical: A novel that takes place in a true-to-life period of history, with emphases on the details of the setting. Sub-genres may include historical thriller, historical horror, and historical romance.

Horror: A story that evokes fear and/or revulsion using supernatural or psychological elements.

Horror Thriller: A thriller/suspense in which the antagonist is a monster-villain and includes graphic violence.

How-To: A book that offers the reader specific instructions, information, and advice to accomplish a goal.

Inverted: A mystery story in which the reader knows who committed the crime.

Legal Thriller: A tale in which the hero is a lawyer who uses his skills to battle the bad guys.

Locked Room: A mystery tale in which the crime is apparently committed under impossible circumstances.

Magical Realism: A horror story where dark forces or creatures exist in real-life settings.

Medical Mystery: A story that involves a medical threat or illegal use of medical technology.

Medical Thriller: Either a tale in which the hero is in the medical profession and uses his skills to battle the antagonist, or a story that features the illegal or immoral use of medical technology.

Memoir: An author's commentary on the people and events that influenced a specific phase of his life.

Military Science Fiction: Tales of war set in the future that incorporate real-life, current-day military technology.

Military Thriller: A story in which the hero is a member of the military working as part of a specialized force.

Multicultural Romance: A romance centered on non-Caucasian characters, most often African-American or Hispanic.

Mundane Science Fiction: Tales that include only scientific knowledge that is known to actually exist.

Mystery Science Fiction: Either a science fiction tale with a central mystery or a classic mystery story with science fiction elements.

Mystery Thriller: A suspense mystery with an international story and lots of action.

Mythic Fiction: Fantasy stories inspired by classic myths, legends, or fairy tales.

New Age (fiction): A fantasy novel that speculates on occult subjects, such as astrology, psychic phenomena, spiritual healing, UFOs, and mysticism.

Paranormal: Includes supernatural elements, such as time travel or characters with psychic abilities.

Police Procedural: A crime thriller or mystery story that focuses on the processes of real-life police procedures and is told from the perspective of the police as they work a case.

Political Intrigue: A thriller in which the hero must ensure the safety of the government.

Post-Apocalyptic: Science fiction tales that focus on the struggle to survive on Earth after an apocalypse.

Private Detective: A mystery in which the crime is solved by a private investigator.

Psychological Horror: A tale based on an insane or psychologically disturbed character who is often a human-monster.

Psychological Suspense: A mystery that focuses on the details of the crime and what motivated the perpetrator to commit the crime.

Psychological Thriller: A suspense that highlights the emotional and mental conflict between the hero and the villain.

Quiet Horror: A story that uses atmosphere and mood to elicit fear and create suspense, rather than graphic description.

Religious Horror: A story that incorporates religious icons and mythology, such as angels and demons.

Religious Sci-Fi/Fantasy: A science fiction or fantasy novel that centers on theological ideas and heroes who are ruled by religious beliefs.

Romance: Novels that feature love stories.

Romance Sci-Fi: A science fiction story in which romance is central to the plot.

Romantic Comedy: A romance focused on humor.

Romantic Mystery: A mystery tale in which the crime-solvers are romantically involved.

Romantic Suspense: A romance tale that includes a heroine who may have to solve a crime or mystery.

Romantic Thriller: A suspense in which the protagonists are romantically involved.

Science Fantasy: A fantasy story in which the fantastical ele-

ments are supported by scientific explanations.

Science Fiction: Novels that incorporate elements of science or pseudo-science.

Science Fiction/Fantasy: A designation used by booksellers to collapse two separate genres into one for marketing purposes.

Science-Fiction Horror: A tale that deals with alien invasions, mad scientists, or out-of-control experiments.

Sensual: A romance story based on the sensual tension between the hero and heroine.

Social Science Fiction: Stories that focus on how characters react to their environments.

Soft Science Fiction: Stories based on softer sciences such as psychology, sociology, and anthropology.

Space Opera: A science fiction tale with traditional heroes and villains, and plenty of action scenes.

Spicy: A romance that involves a married couple.

Splatter/Splatterpunk: A horror novel that presents extremely explicit scenes and gruesome violence.

Spy-Fi: Espionage stories with science fiction elements, such as high-tech gadgets.

Steampunk: A sci-fi/fantasy tale that presents an alternate history in which characters in Victorian England have access to 20th century technology.

Superheroes: Fantasy or science fiction tale featuring characters with superhuman abilities.

Supernatural Menace: A horror story featuring supernatural elements, such as ghosts, demons, vampires, and werewolves, which cause mayhem.

Supernatural Thriller: A suspense in which the hero or the antagonist (or both) have supernatural powers.

Suspense: Novels that use elements of suspense to solve a crime or unravel a mystery.

Sweet: A romance with a heroine who is a virgin.

Sword and Sorcery: A classic fantasy tale set in medieval period that incorporates wizardry.

Technological Thriller: A suspense in which out-of-control technology is central to the plot.

Technology Horror: A horror tale that features technology out of control.

Technothriller: A thriller mystery that emphasizes high technology.

Thriller: A novel that uses suspense to tell the story and incorporates a plot structure that focuses gamesmanship and centers on hunt-and-chase scenes.

Thriller Science Fiction: A sci-fi novel that incorporates elements of a classic thriller story.

Time-Travel: Science fiction tales based on the concept of moving backward or forward through time and into parallel worlds.

Urban Fantasy: A story in which characters with magical powers appear in a normal modern setting (similar to magical realism).

Vampire Fantasy: A fantasy novel that incorporates the classic vampire story, focusing on sexuality and romantic liaisons, without the horror elements.

Weird Tales: A horror tale that features strange and uncanny events.

Western: a story set in the North American, South American, or Australian west.

Woman in Jeopardy: A mystery story in which the heroine is placed in peril by a crime and struggles to triumph over the perpetrator.

Wuxia: Fantasy stories that incorporate martial arts and Chinese philosophies.

Young Adult: Books written specifically for teenagers, ages 12 to 17, with heroes the same age as the readers.

Young Adult Horror: Horror stories that are written specifically for teenagers; they include heroes who are young adults and are less violent than traditional horror tales.

Young Adult Mystery: Mystery stories written specifically for teenagers; they include a young adult hero detective who pursues criminals who are usually less violent than those in adult mystery novels.

Young Adult Romance: A romance written specifically for teenagers; they include a hero and heroine who are young adults and contain very little sexual content.

Zombie: Horror tales featuring dead people who come "alive" and torment the living.

The Six Large Publishing Houses and Their Imprints

PUBLISHER: HarperCollins	
HarperCollins General Books	Harper Perennial
Amistad	Harper Perennial Modern Classics
Avon	HarperAudio
Avon A	HarperCollins
Avon Red	HarperCollins e-Books
Caedom	Harper Entertainment
Collins	HarperLuxe
Collins Design	HarperSanFrancisco
Dark Alley	HarperTorch
Ecco	Morrow Cookbooks
Eos	Rayo
Harper Paperbacks	William Morrow

PUBLISHER: Random House

Bantam Dell Publishing Group

Bantam Hardcover

Bantam Mass Market

Bantam Trade Paperback

Crimeline

Delacorte Press

Dell

Delta

Domain

DTP

Fanfare

Island

Spectra

The Dial Press

Crown Publishing Group

Clarkson Potter

Crown Business

Crown Publishers, Inc.

Harmony Books

Potter Style

Potter Craft

Shaye Arehart Books

Three Rivers Press

Knopf Publishing Group

Alfred A. Knopf

Anchor Books

Everyman's Library

Pantheon Books

Schoken Books

Vintage Books

Doubleday Broadway Publishing Group

Broadway Books

Currency Doubleday

Doubleday Image

Doubleday Religious Publishing

Harlem Moon

Main Street Books

Morgan Road Books

Speigel & Grau

Nan A. Talese

Random House Publishing Group

Ballantine Books

Del Rey

Del Rey / Lucas Books

Fawcett

Ivy

The Modern Library

One World

Random House Trade Group

Random House Trade Paperbacks

Reader's Circle

Striver's Row Books

Villard Books

Wellspring

PUBLISHER: Harlequin

Harlequin

Harlequin American Romance

Harlequin Bianca

Harlequin Blaze

Harlequin Deseo

Harlequin Everlasting Love

Harlequin Ginger Blossom

Harlequin Historical

Harlequin Intrigue

Harlequin Jazmin

Harlequin Julia

Harlequin Medical romance

Harlequin NEXT

Harlequin Presents

Harlequin Romance

Harlequin Superromance

HQN Books

LUNA

Mills & Boon

Mills & Boon Historical Romance

Mills & Boon Medical Romance

Mills & Boon Modern Xtra-Sensual

MIRA

Kimani Press

Arabesque Inspirational Romance

Arabesque Romance

Kimani Romance

Kimani TRU

Kimani Press New Spirit

Kimani Press Romance Sepia

Red Dress Ink

Silhouette

Silhouette Bombshell

Silhouette Desire

Silhouette Nocturne

Silhouette Romance

Silhouette Romantic Suspense

Silhouette Special Edition

SPICE

Steeple Hill

Steeple Hill Café

Steeple Hill Love Inspired

Steeple Hill Love Inspired Historical

Steeple Hill Live Inspired Suspense

Steeple Hill Women's Fiction

PUBLISHER: Holtzbrinck Publishers

Farrar, Straus & Giroux

Faber & Faber, Inc.

Farrar, Straus & Giroux for Young Readers

Hill & Wang

North Point Press

Henry Holt and Co. LLC

Books for Young Readers

Metropolitan Books

Owl Books

Times books

Pan MacMillan

Boxtree

MacMillan

MacMillan Children's Books

Pan

Picador

Siggwick & Jackson

St. Martin's Press

Griffin Books

Let's Go

Minotaur

St. Martin's Paperbacks

St. Martin's Press

Thomas Dunne Books

Truman Talley Books

Tom Doherty Associates

Forge

Tor Books

PUBLISHER: PenguinGroup USA

Ace Books

Alpha Books

Avery

Berkeley Books

Dutton

Gotham Books

HPBooks

Hudson Street Press

Jeremy P. Tarcher

Jove

New American Library

Penguin

Penguin Press

Perigree

Plume

Portfolio

Putnam

Riverhead Books

Sentinel

Viking

PUBLISHER: Simon & Schuster	
Atrria Books	Scribner
Free Press	Simon & Schuster
Howard Books	Strebor
Pocket Books	The Touchstone & Fireside Group

Glossary of Terms

Advance: Payments made to a writer by the publisher prior to the book's publication. An advance is calculated against the estimated future sales of the book and is usually paid in installments.

Artwork: These are elements of a book that require graphic design.

Author's Voice or Author's Style: The unique way a writer uses words and phrases to tell a story that distinguishes the author from other writers.

Back Cover: This refers to the back cover of a book.

Book Dealer: A business that acquires books from publishers and sells them to consumers.

Book Distribution: The method of getting books from the publisher's warehouse into bookstores and other retail outlets.

Book Proposal: A detailed presentation of a nonfiction book's concept and marketing potential. It is used to acquire an agent and sell a book idea to a publisher.

Book Reviewer: A person who provides critiques and evaluations of literary works.

Copy Editing: The act of reviewing a manuscript to ensure accuracy in writing style, grammar, punctuation, and arrangement.

Copyright: The legal right of ownership of a written work.

Credentials: Items that provide proof of one's education, experience, or expertise.

Dust Jacket: This is an outer detachable cover (made of paper) of a hardcover book.

Editor: A person who works at a publishing house, acquires projects, and coordinates the process of publication.

Endorsement or Testimonial: A written statement praising the content of the book.

Exclusive: Offering a manuscript or book proposal to only one agent for a set period and guaranteeing no one else may consider it during the exclusivity period.

Film Rights: Rights sold or optioned by an agent to allow a book to be made into a film.

Foreign Rights: Rights that allow the book to be reprinted or translated outside the United States.

Foreword: A front section of a book written by an expert in the field or a celebrity to introduce the topic.

Galleys: Copies of the book's interior layout for proofing prior to print.

Genre: A classification of literature by common elements, styles, or themes.

Imprint: The name used to identify a publisher's specific line of books. Imprints are separate lines of products within a publishing house.

Interior Layout: The design of the inside of the book; including placement of chapter titles, images, and other material.

ISBN (International Standard Book Number): A ten-digit number that is linked to and identifies the title and publisher of a book. It appears on the back of all books, as well as the dust jacket and the copyright page.

Library of Congress Catalog Number: A number used by the Library of Congress to identify books it includes in its collection. Libraries use this number to order and catalog books.

Literary Agent: A person who acts on behalf of an author to sell his or her book to a publisher, negotiate contracts, and deal with subsidiary rights. Though agents are not lawyers, their experience working with publishing agreements provides the necessary knowledge to negotiate contracts for their clients.

Marketing Department: This is a department in the publishing house consisting of professionals who are responsible for promoting and selling books.

Multiple Submissions: Submitting several pitches for different projects to one agent at the same time. Agents will reject an author who sends multiple submissions.

Novel: A fiction book.

One-Time Rights: Rights that allow a portion of a book to be published again (for instance, in a magazine) without violating the contract.

Option Clause: A clause in a contract granting the publisher the right to release an author's subsequent books.

Platform: A writer's media exposure and abilities to develop a potential group of readers. This is accomplished through blogs, speaking engagements, and interviews.

Popular Trend: A topic that is currently favored by a large percentage of people.

Potential Sales: The forecasted number of books the publisher believes it can reasonably expect to sell.

Print on Demand (POD): Copies of books printed to order.

Promotional Plan: An author's strategy to market and publicize his book.

Publisher: The company that releases and publishes a book.

Query Letter: A letter submitted to an agent to pitch the author and garner interest in a book project.

Reprint Rights: The right to republish a book after its initial print run.

Royalties: A percentage of the retail price that is paid to the author for each copy of the book that is sold.

SASE: A self-addressed, stamped envelope.

Self-publishing: A publishing project that requires the author to pay for the costs of manufacturing, distributing, and marketing the book.

Serial Rights: The rights granted to a magazine or paper to publish a portion of a book.

Simultaneous Submission: Submitting the same query letter, manuscript, or book proposal to several agents at the same time.

Solicited: A manuscript or book proposal that has been requested by the agent.

Subsidiary Rights: All rights, except for book publishing rights, listed in a publishing contract. These may include book club rights, paperback rights, and film rights.

Synopsis: A summary of the main plot points, characters, and storyline of a fiction manuscript.

Timely and Relevant: When a topic has significance to current events or trends.

Titles: A publisher's portfolio of books.

Typeface: A specific font.

University Press: A publishing house affiliated with a sponsoring university.

Unsolicited: A manuscript or book proposal sent to an agent without prior permission.

UPC (Universal Product Code) Bar Code: a 12-number code imprinted on retail products (including books) to track trade items.

Successful Query
Letters and Synopses

SUCCESSFUL QUERY LETTER: NAR-
RATIVE NONFICTION

October 29, 2008

Dear Mr. Mosely:

It was pleasure meeting you at the Writer's Digest Conference last month and learning that you represent historical nonfiction.

There's one oddity of Western history, it is that it is often difficult to tell the difference between the good guys and the bad guys.

Billy the Kid and Pat Garrett straddle the line between good and evil... and misunderstood. History tells the story of William H. Bonnie as a homicidal psychopath and Sheriff Pat Garrett as the dirty coward who shot him in the back.

But that's not the real story. ETERNAL DESPERADO will explore the myth and the folklore surrounding these two men and analyze the crimes of the Lincoln County War in the context of the political corruption of the New Mexico Territory in the late 1800s.

The book will reveal how the legends were deliberately manufactured and manipulated to divert attention from larger crimes committed by politicians and powerful businessmen. ETERNAL DESPERADO is a 90,000-word narrative nonfiction that will set the record straight and introduce readers to the outlaws and lawmen of the Old West. These stories are as relevant today as they were 125 years ago.

I am the author of 12 published books, recipient of the Western History Alive honor and the award for Outstanding Achievement in Western History, and I hold a master's degree in history of the southwest. I write the popular blog "Western Outlaws and Lawmen," which receives more than 50,000 visitors each month. I also host the weekly television program "Welcome to the Old West" that is syndicated nationally, and I lecture at universities throughout the United States and Europe, speaking to more than 250,000 people each year.

Thank you for taking the time to ready my query. I have a completed book proposal and manuscript available for your review, should you be interested in the project. I look forward to the possibility of working together.

Sincerely,

Thomas Tyler
1234 Main Street
Anywhere USA, 11111
(505) 555-5555
Thomas@emailaddress.com

SUCCESSFUL QUERY LETTER: MEMOIR

Dear Ms. Gardner:

I was born and raised in the Fundamentalist Church of Jesus Christ of Latter-Day Saints, which was lead by Warren Jeffs and whose compound in Eldorado, Texas, was recently raided. In this raid they have removed more than 400 women and children they believe to be under abuse or eminent threat of abuse. These events have been dominating the headlines for the past week now. As events unfold, the public is becoming increasingly curious about what life is like inside this cult.

There are other books that have been written about life inside polygamist cults like the FLDS Church and they have become bestsellers. Irene Spencer (my aunt) wrote *Shattered Dreams*, which is a bestseller. *Carolyn Jessop's Escape* is also another popular book on the subject.

What makes my book stand out is that it is the first of its kind from the perspective of a young man growing up in a polygamist cult. It is not full of dark stories of abuse, although abuse is addressed in it. It is filled with stories of the humorous things that were part of being in a large family like ours. The goal is to make the reader fall in love with my family before dealing with the abuses, so the impact on the reader's emotions is greater. It is also an inspirational Christian story about the healing power of Christ to reconcile the pains of the past. It is about how I could eventually see my value through Christ's eyes and to be able to put the past behind me, even to the point of being able to forgive my own father, who was an abuser and pedophile.

The book begins in the office of my psychiatrist where I am seeking help to keep from acting on my homicidal thoughts and feelings toward my father. I use the psychiatrist's office to explain my family's background in Mormonism (I am a seventh generation Mormon) and how the FLDS Mormons came to be. I then use a flashback to present my life growing up in this cult. Toward the end I come back to the psychiatrist's office where he helps me come to grips with my feelings and I move on from there in real-time.

I get married, have a son, and then come to faith in Christ where I learn the power of forgiveness so profoundly that it compels me to forgive my father. The book ends with the events surrounding my father's funeral and the conclusions that I draw from it.

I look forward to hearing from you.

Yours truly,
Brian J. Mackert

SUCCESSFUL QUERY LETTER: NONFICTION ANTHOLOGY

Dear Mr. Sternfeld,

"Well-behaved women rarely make history," Laurel Thatcher Ulrich.

That's because well-behaved women don't rescue men in the Wild West, discover Radium, or achieve Hollywood stardom after being fired from countless chorus-line jobs. Well-behaved women don't speed 300 miles/hour around a racetrack, trek in the Egyptian desert in full Victorian garb – and they certainly don't soar into the mysterious unknown.

Several biographies describe women who didn't behave and made history – but few anthologies provide real-life applications for readers.

What can we learn from the divas, outlaws and entrepreneurs who pursued their passions? What do they have that many of us lack? Juice, life force, energy, passion, vision, and the ability to embrace change. We have juice, but life drains it. We have dreams, but our mothers, partners, kids, jobs, and our own personalities can override them. We get rejected, depressed, anxious and scared — and we stop living even though we're still breathing.

SEE JANE SOAR! 200 WHO WEREN'T WELL-BEHAVED:
FOLLOWING THEIR HEARTS, MAKING HISTORY:

- Presents brief, accurate profiles of historical and contemporary women from all cultures and nationalities.

- Emphasizes personality traits, achievements, and struggles. Each profile includes quotes from the woman and direct life applications for the reader.

- Highlights 10 different categories: outlaws, divas, athletes, politicians, explorers, entrepreneurs, etc.. Readers can easily access subjects that interest them.

This book offers more than a link to history. It inspires women to change and grow, to achieve their goals – whether that means earning a Ph.D., losing that last 10 pounds, or asking for a bank loan. Readers will see themselves in the lives of these women who courageously pursued their talents and dreams. They'll learn that Annie Oakley didn't shoot photographs and Annie Leibovitz didn't shoot targets because they followed their own hearts, minds, and souls.

SEE JANE SOAR will encourage women to accept and nurture who they truly are.

SEE JANE SOAR has the potential to morph into a calendar or daily journal for holiday or first-day-of-school gifts. A "soar" series is possible: 200 girls who didn't behave and changed history – or 200 Canadians, seniors, athletes, teachers, people with disabilities, people with diseases, and so on.

My degrees in Education and Psychology give me a solid background with which to research and write this book. I lived and taught in Africa for three years and traveled worldwide – I know how exciting it is to soar!

And I write. My publications include articles for *Woman's Day, Flare, Reader's Digest, Glow, alive, Esteem, Good Times, Today's Health* and *Wellness*, and *cahoots*. Let me know if you'd like to review a full book proposal.

Yours truly,
Laurie Pawlik-Kienlen

SUCCESSFUL QUERY LETTER: HOW-TO (PRACTICAL) NONFICTION

Gina Cunningham
1234 Main Street
Anywhere USA, 11111
(555) 555-5555 / gina@emailaddress.com

August 3, 2002

Ms. Angela Miller
The Miller Agency
300 West Broadway
New York, NY 10013

Dear Ms. Miller:

I found your listing in the "Guide to Literary Agents" and I am interested in the possibility of working together. I have an idea for a how-to nonfiction book titled MODERN TRADITIONS: INSPIRING IDEAS FOR INCORPORATING YESTERDAY'S CUSTOMS INTO TODAY'S WEDDINGS.

This book will be the first to present cultural wedding customs with a twist: updated and reinterpreted for today's couples. I will provide inspiring suggestions on how couples can use these traditional elements in a modern way to personalize their wedding, honor their roots, and create a stylish celebration. Vibrant photographs of design elements, idea boxes, celebrity wedding references, and real couples' stories will be woven throughout the text.

As a celebrated wedding designer, coordinator, and owner of Wedding Design Studio in Los Angeles, I create and produce distinctive weddings for couples. My diverse portfolio includes both celebrity couples (actors and prominent sports figures) and everyday couples. I have been featured on several episodes of Lifetime Television's "Weddings of a Lifetime," The Today Show, and Good Morning, America. I author a bi-monthly column on theme weddings in *Inside Weddings Magazine* and speak to more than 50,000 event professionals at conferences each year. My blog, Designing Poetic Weddings, receives more than 5,000 hits per day and I have a database of 85,000 subscribers for my monthly e-news-letter. I have been featured in *Elegant Bride Magazine, Bridal Guide, Conde Nast Bride's WeddingBells, The Knot WeddingPages, InStyle Magazine, Martha Stewart Weddings,* and *The Los Angeles Times.*

I have a completed proposal and sample chapter I can send to you. Please let me know if you are interested in the book.

Thank you for your time and consideration.

Sincerely,

Gina Cunningham

SUCCESSFUL QUERY LETTER: URBAN FANTASY

Dear Ms. Pepus,

I found your Web site on WritersDigest.com and thought you may be interested in my novel. After reviewing your wish list, I thought you might enjoy this slice of urban fantasy.

In brief, Shiarra Waynest is a private detective working in an alternate, present-day New York City. Less than ten years ago, creatures such as vampires, werewolves, and magi (collectively called "Others") have come out of the closet and are now vying for equal rights and the same protection under the law as any other human being. As most any human would be, Shiarra is trying to come to grips with these changes while still making ends meet. A mage contacts Shiarra and essentially gives her an offer she can't resist. For a good sum of money that just may be enough to save her failing PI firm, she agrees to work with a coven of magi to find where a local vampire, Alec Royce, has hidden a powerful artifact.

What Shiarra doesn't count on is the depth of corruption in the mage coven, how the vampire Royce is not what he seems, and having to deal with and solve the murder of supernaturals that seem to come in contact with the focus. It is primarily about her getting in way over her head, far too fast, and having to find a way to save herself, and later her friends from the corruption of the focus.

HUNTED BY THE OTHERS is an 83,000-word work of mystery/urban fantasy with a touch of humor. I can supply a full transcript at request. This is my first novel, and I anticipate being able to expand into a series.

Thank you very much for taking the time to read my query. I have included the first couple of chapters for your consideration below. I hope to hear from you soon.

Best regards,
Jess Haines

SUCCESSFUL QUERY LETTER: COZY MYSTERY

Dear Ms. Faust,

I enjoyed meeting you at the conference in Austin this past weekend. As I mentioned, I have had my eye on BookEnds for quite some time; when I discovered you would be at the conference, I knew I had to attend. We met during the final pitch session and discussed how the series I am working on might fit in with your current line of mysteries. Per your request, I have enclosed a synopsis and the first three chapters of MURDER ON THE ROCKS, an 80,000-word cozy mystery that was a finalist in this year's Writers' League of Texas manuscript contest and includes several bed-and-breakfast recipes.

Thirty-eight-year-old Natalie Barnes has quit her job, sold her house, and gambled everything she has on the Gray Whale Inn on Cranberry Island, Maine. But she's barely fired up the stove when portly developer Bernard Katz rolls into town and starts mowing through her morning glory muffins. Natalie needs the booking, but Katz is hard to stomach — especially when he unveils his plan to build an oversized golf resort on top of the endangered tern colony next door. When the town board approves the new development, not only do the terns face extinction, but Natalie's Inn might just follow. Just when Natalie thinks she can't face more trouble, she discovers Katz's body at the base of the cliff and becomes the police's No. 1 suspect. If Natalie doesn't find the killer fast she stands to lose everything — maybe even her life.

I am a former pubic relations writer, a graduate of Rice University, a member of the Writers' League of Texas, and founder of the Austin Mystery Writers critique group. I have spent many summers in fishing communities in Maine and Newfoundland, and escape to Maine as often as possible. The second Gray Whale Inn mystery, DEAD AND BERRIED, is currently in the computer.

If you would like to see the manuscript, I can be reached at (phone number). Thank you for your time and attention; I look forward to hearing from you soon.

Sincerely,
Karen Swartz MacInerney

SUCCESSFUL QUERY LETTER: CHRISTIAN LITERARY FICTION

Dear Victoria:

What happens when a lost man finds Christ, only to lose his soul?

The first person novel, MAMMOTH MOUNTAIN (100,000 words) is a cross between *The Catcher in the Rye* and *Good Will Hunting*. Set in the early 1980s, it follows four years in the life of Drew, a pot smoking, thieving, womanizer who's coming to terms with his violent upbringing by an alcoholic father, a man who may not be his biological father.

Twenty-one years old and new to Mammoth he continually brawls with a powerful Olympic ski racer, but has an even more dangerous nemesis inside his head. Over four years, Drew's roller coaster life takes him to the Pacific Northwest, Maui, and Mexico, but he always returns to Mammoth Mountain. With the help of an old friend, he barely pulls through his mental breakdown in a cave on Maui and becomes a father himself, vowing to do a better job than his father did.

MAMMOTH MOUNTAIN is a "Rated R" Christian novel.

I have had more than twenty stories and editorials published in: *The San Diego Union Tribune*, *The Surfer's Journal*, *Surfer Magazine*, and *Surfing Magazine*. My collection of short stories, *Zen and the Art of Surfing* is now in its eighth printing. In 1998, five of the stories were originally published in *The Surfer's Journal* (20,000 copies) and the Julian Paz Foundation now publishes the entire collection through a grant. There are currently three magazines that are going to run more stories from the collection: *SurfMor* (a new magazine), *The Surfer's Path* (based in the U.K.) and *Ocean* magazine. You can read an excerpt of the collection at my Web site and I'd be happy to send you a copy of *Zen and the Art of Surfing*.

Sincerely,

Greg Guttierez

SUCCESSFUL QUERY LETTER: HISTORICAL CHILDREN'S FICTION

Dear Ms. Adams,

I attended the SCBWI National Conference in New York in February, and was delighted to hear of your interest in historical fiction. Please find the first three chapters of SELLING HOPE, a historical novel, attached.

Hope McDaniels wants to break free from the vaudeville circuit, and she sees opportunity blazing toward her in the nighttime sky: Halley's Comet. On May 19, 1910, Earth will pass through the tail of Halley's Comet. Many believe this to be the end of days. Hope believes this to be her jackpot...

The passing of Earth through the tail of Halley's Comet has been described as the world's first case of mass hysteria. The "abundant" media, combined with the clashing of holdover Victorian sensibilities with Industrial-age objectivity, created a spark that made May 1910, one very interesting month.

My middle-grade historical novel, *Autumn Winifred Oliver Does Things Different*, will be released this October by Delacorte Press. I've also penned more than a dozen activity books for children, many for licensed characters like Scooby-Doo, Lisa Frank, PowerPuff Girls, and Holly Hobbie. I won the *Highlights Magazine* Pewter Plate award for Outstanding Arts Feature for "They'll Be Back," a story that appeared in the June 2005 issue of *Highlights*. My work has also appeared in *Guideposts for Kids* and *Spider Magazine*.

After reviewing your Web site, I was excited to see that your goal is to represent authors, not books. In that regard, I feel our goals are similar, and hope that we'll have the opportunity to work together.

All the best,

Kristin O'Donnell Tubb

SUCCESSFUL QUERY LETTER: HUMOROUS PARANORMAL

Dear Ms. Faust,

Straight-laced preschool teacher, Lizzie Brown, never lies, never cusses, and doesn't really care much for surprises. When her long lost Grandma Gertie shows up on her doorstep riding a neon pink Harley David-son wearing a "kiss my asphalt" T-shirt and hauling a carpet bag full of Smucker's jars filled with road kill magic, Lizzie doesn't think her life could get any stranger. That is, until her hyperactive terrier starts talking and an ancient demon decides to kill her from his perch on the back of her toilet.

Lizzie learns she's a demon slayer, fated to square off with the devil's top minion in, oh about two weeks. Sadly, she's untrained, unfit, and under at-tack. Grandma's gang of fifty-something biker witches promises to whip Lizzie into shape, as long as she joins them out on the road. But Lizzie wants nothing to do with all this craziness. She simply wants her normal life back. When she accidentally botches the spell meant to protect her, she only has one choice — trust the utterly delicious but secretive man who claims to be her protector.

Dimitri Kallinikos has had enough. Cursed by a demon centuries ago, his formerly prominent clan has dwindled down to himself and his younger twin sisters, both of whom are now in the coma that precedes certain death. To break the curse, he must kill the demon behind it. Dimitri needs a slayer. At long last, he's found Lizzie. But how do you talk a girl you've never met into going straight to Hell? Lie (and hope she forgives you). Dimitri decides to pass himself off as Lizzie's fated protector in or-der to gain her trust and guide her toward this crucial mission. But will his choice to deceive her cost them their lives, or simply their hearts?

THE ACCIDENTAL DEMON SLAYER is an 85,000 word humorous paranormal. I'm a member of RWA and the partial manuscript placed first in the Windy City RWA's Four Seasons contest.

The judge for that contest, Leah Hultenschmidt of Dorchester Publishing, has just requested the full. As an advertising writer, I've won multiple awards for my work in radio dialogue.

I would be happy to send you the complete manuscript. Thank you for your consideration and time.

Sincerely,

Angie Fox Gwinner

SUCCESSFUL QUERY LETTER: EROTIC ROMANCE

(This is a follow-up to an initial query that resulted in a request for a synopsis and chapters.)

Dear Ms. Faust:

Thank you for responding to my e-mail query so quickly! Here are the first five chapters and synopsis for MINE, ALL MINE, a single title erotic romance that is a perfect fit for Kensington Brava. I believe your agency would be ideal for representing the project.

MINE, ALL MINE is the erotic story of desire, passion, and unrequited love in San Francisco and the rolling hills of Tuscany. Lily Ellis has been deeply in lust with Travis Carson for well over a decade. But since Travis likes his women bold and sassy, not meek and size 14, she knows her feelings will never be anything more than bathtub fantasies with Travis's name on her lips. But all it takes is one special night at a fashion show in San Francisco, one very special dress, and the wonders of Tuscany to change Travis's feelings for Lily forever.

My first novel, *Authors in Ecstasy* (published by Ellora's Cave under the pseudonym Bella Andre), received a 4.5 star review in the March 2004 edition of Romantic Times magazine.

My publishing experience also includes several novellas with Ellora's Cave and two non-fiction books on the music business. I am a member of RWA and a graduate of Stanford University.

Thank you for your consideration. I look forward to hearing from you.

Sincerely,

Bella Andre

SUCCESSFUL SYNOPSIS: MODERN ROMANCE NOVEL

(Mail version)

1234 Main street
Anywhere, USA
(555) 555-5555
me@mye-mail.com

TENDER HARVEST

By Kimberly Llewellyn

Synopsis

Sally's Story...

After inheriting her parents' ailing cranberry bogs, SALLY JOHNSON must come home to save Misty Meadows. In doing so, she leaves behind a lucrative career, a condo, and an ex-husband who gambled away her life savings. But how can she succeed at saving the bogs when she discovers that some mysterious Wall Street whiz kid will arrive soon with a different set of plans for the bogs? She's immediately wary about meeting her late father's "silent partner."

Several past experiences, some that even go back several generations, has taught Sally well that she can trust no one and has only herself to depend on. She shares these feelings with CASSO, who has always been like a second dad to her. Casso is a Thoreau-wanna-be, who's lived on and loved the bogs for twenty years. He was also her dad's best friend.

To make matters worse for Sally, when this mysterious, worldly Wall Street hotshot shows up, he turns out to be TAIGN McCLORY, the first man she's ever loved... and lost.

Taign's Story...

Ten years ago, Taign McClory left town as a rebel.

Today, he returns to Pequot, Massachusetts, as a money mogul. He had his own painful, personal reasons for becoming a silent partner to Sally's father and trying to financially save the cranberry bogs. Despite secretly hoping that the bogs would bring him back to Sally one day, he never dreamed it would be under these lousy circumstances.

He's worked hard to become the kind of man that Sally deserves. He's no longer the troubled tough kid who skipped town the night the fateful brush fires destroyed the town's land... including part of Sally's beloved cranberry bogs. He'd broken Sally's heart once before when he rejected her plea to stay and clear his name, and now he has to hurt her all over again when he must get rid of the last thing she has left of her parents — Misty Meadows. Not like he's got much of a choice.

But so much more than just his savings has been tied up in the bogs. Helping to finance the bogs was Taign's secret way of making up for the brush fires so long ago. Although he's never told Sally, Taign has always felt responsible for those brush fires. After all, he should have been able to stop his old man, who had set them in a drunken rage. But his father has since died and can never hurt another soul again. Taign has never revealed the truth about his father's role in the fires. Pride prevents him from telling a soul (not even Sally) because it would mean revealing the painful secret of his father's physical abuse.

The Story Opens...

The emotional tug of war between Sally and Taign is immediate when they both have opposing plans for Misty Meadows. What makes things impossible for Sally is seeing Taign again. His mere presence stirs up long-buried emotions. But her last memory of him is all too clear — she told him she'd stick by his side if he stayed and faced the town's accusations, but he flatly refused.

Taign remembers that night all too well. He had no choice but to refuse her plea to stay. After all, the town and its cranberry bogs were going up in flames and he secretly believed it was his fault. He'd worked for Sally's father, the only man in town to ever give him a chance. After feeling responsible for the loss of part of the man's bogs, he couldn't steal his daughter's heart, too. Instead, he left Pequot.

Llewellyn/TENDER HARVEST/Synopsis   **3**

Today, Taign quickly realizes how much Misty Meadows still means to Sally, and to him. Seeing Sally again makes his senses go haywire. He has a change of heart about selling. With the cranberry harvest around the corner, he decides to stay and help save the cranberry bogs somehow in a last-ditch effort to make things right with her.

But Sally's not happy with Taign's decision at first. Not if it means he'll always be underfoot, making her confront her unresolved feelings about him. His constant nearness stirs up youthful emotions within her to the point where she can't think straight. Can she learn to risk trusting this man once again when trusting anyone has only caused heartache?

Harvesting the bogs comes with its share of problems; equipment has been woefully neglected, others suspiciously broken. A lifelong rival of Sally's dad insists that the land be sold to him. A woman from Taign's past makes trouble. Worst of all, Sally's best friend, FAITH — along with Casso — keep trying to play cupid! Despite these obstacles, nothing can seem to stop the growing feelings between Sally and Taign.

Constantly thrown together, Sally and Taign can no longer deny their growing affection. Sally finds herself sharing a kiss with Taign. However, she must overcome emotional obstacles that keep her heart from falling for him again too fast. She still needs to know the entire truth about the night of the fires... the very night Taign left town. She also needs to hear why he didn't return to her one day, the way he'd promised so long ago..

Llewellyn/TENDER HARVEST/Synopsis   **4**

Taign finally must confront his past and admits to Sally his role in the brush fires. He blames himself for his dad's behavior back then and tells Sally how he had desperately tried to stop the fires that night. But he'd failed. Sally reads between the lines and understands that Taign hadn't been the cause of the brush fires. He'd merely been a victim of circumstance, despite his guilt and belief that he'd been responsible. She urges him to come to grips with his past. She also states she'll keep her promise and stand by him once again as he faces the townspeople and clears his name. She can no longer deny that she never stopped caring for him. Taign confesses to her that he's dreamed about this moment…to be back in her life and to tell her the truth about that fateful night.

But contentment between the two is fleeting once Sally remembers that Taign will eventually be returning to New York. She fears she's lost her heart to him and he would leave her once again for good. Also, problems with the cranberry bogs worsen; Taign admits that he doesn't think the bogs will survive unless he keeps his New York job to support the place. He confesses that things look worse for the bogs and doesn't see how Sally will ever turn the place around despite her noble intentions. He does say however, that he's just happy to help her try and keep Misty Meadows as long as possible. He may have to keep his job in New York, but he promises he isn't ever going to leave her.

Although Sally must come to grips with the realization that she will probably lose her family's land, she does finally trust (and is delighted) that Taign will not abandon her. But her trust in Taign is shaken when she finds a Letter of Intent to sell off some of the land to Sally's father's rival, the one man she'd never sell out to. Betrayed, she confronts Taign about this secret letter.

Taign truly believes he's doing the right thing by selling his half to the neighboring berry grower. At least Sally will keep a portion of her land and her home. Sally does believe his honest intentions, but pleads with him that it's the wrong thing to do and to give her more time. He agrees to hold off as long as possible. Although she believes Taign's heart in the right place, his actions painfully remind Sally that she doesn't have control over her own destiny.

But Sally then discovers that Taign has sacrificed everything to save Misty Meadows the best he can. He's done so much more than provide a mere minor financial investment. He's risked losing his job, ending his career, and bankrupting his entire portfolio (heck, he's even about to sell off his SUV). He hasn't revealed any of this to her. He's doing it all for this one harvest alone…and he's doing all for her, to make up for the past. She realizes that he has indeed become a man worthy of her trust and admits she loves him for it.

But she can't allow both of them to lose their livelihoods. She loves him too much to allow that to happen. He's worked too hard to throw it all away just to rectify the past with her. Unable to sleep one night, she decides she must sacrifice her love for him and she must make him go back to New York after all.

Heartbroken, she gets up and attempts to send him packing by trying to sign the Letter of Intent. She won't let Taign throw his entire life away. But Taign stops her. In a late night argument, she tells him that she knows he's going to lose everything and demands that he leave before he makes that costly mistake. But he won't listen to reason and refuses to let her sign the letter. He explains that he won't give up yet... it took him all these years to come back to Misty Meadows and he won't lose her now. Deep down, he always knew the real reason he had to get back to the bogs... to be with her. He never stopped loving Sally. He takes the letter and hides it so she can't sign it.

While he's out of the room, a flicker of light appears through the darkness in the kitchen window and catches Sally's eye. From inside the main house, she peers out the window to see suspicious activity of a flashlight around the harvesting equipment down at the flooded bogs outside. As Taign is in the other room momentarily, she frantically tugs on a jacket, grabs a flashlight, and rushes out into the night to catch the perpetrator, who may be the culprit behind all the mysterious problems.

She catches the culprit. It's Casso! Her deceased father's oldest, dearest friend! He'd been behind all the problems and vandalism at the bogs. But the man had always been like a second father to her. She demands to know why he'd do such a thing as sabotage all the equipment.

Startled by Sally, the older, heavyset man stumbles back, accidentally turning on the tall "cranberry elevator's" conveyor belt that raises into the air about twenty feet. He admits he's been "helping along" the pesky problems as a way to keep Sally and Taign together to prevent the sale of Misty Meadows. He knew her father would want it that way. Besides, it's his home, too, and is desperate not to lose it. He knows Taign's feelings about realistically having to sell the place. And when Casso happened to see the Letter of Intent to sell earlier, he knew he had to do something drastic to buy more time.

Demanding to know more answers, Sally tries to help up the stumbling older man. But soon her jacket gets caught in the chain of the conveyor belt of the moving cranberry elevator and she's dragged high into the air. Before Sally reaches the very top, however, Taign arrives in time to turn off the machinery. Nevertheless, Sally helplessly plummets into darkness.

Sally wakes up in the hospital. Despite the broken arm and cracked collarbone, she's thrilled to see Taign by her side. She admits she doesn't want to lose him. He admits that everything he's accomplished in his life was for one thing — to bring him back to Sally one day. The bogs will always be in his blood, as it is in hers.

He wants to stay at Misty Meadows and offers an attempt at resolving their problems, an idea that Sally would never have accepted before. It's a solution that forces her to learn to finally trust others. She chooses to start by trusting Taign and believes in his decisions, something she wasn't capable of doing before. Taign says he doesn't care if he loses everything now. He tells her that she is everything to him. He tells her he loves her and asks her to marry him and be in his life forever. She happily says yes, but warns him, "This time, Taign McClory, I'm not ever letting you go."

SUCCESSFUL SYNOPSIS: CHICK-LIT NOVEL

(E-mail version)

TULLE LITTLE, TULLE LATE

By Kimberly Llewellyn

Life's Too Short — And So Are My Skirts

A Very Funny, Very Sexy, Very Newfangled Chicklitty Book

Synopsis

"Life's too short and so are my skirts" is the new motto for NINA ROBERTSON after she realizes she's been putting her current life on hold, waiting for her "real" life to begin. Life is what's been happening while she was off making pre-marital plans, which fell through the butt cracks of reality. With the help of her gal-pals, she decides to set a new plan in motion. Her friendships with the gal-pals are genuine… in the sense that they all love each other, but don't necessarily always get along, which is closer to the real thing, right? Who needs brainless-but-supportive cheerleader friends, anyway? Their relationships are the kind where alliances are formed, friendships broken, secrets betrayed, and lives altered forever… and this is all during happy hour!

Right… back to Nina's grand plan. First, she must stop pining over her ex-fiance, JEREMIAH, the famous jet-setting journalist who broke her heart… twice. ("I didn't let him go… he chewed off his own arm and ran!") Then she's gotta start playing "catch-up" with career, friendships, and sex. She must cultivate herself for a change. But can this just-turned-thirty-year-old succeed at getting up to speed and on the fast track without crashing and burning from life's — ahem — little detours? (Oh yeah, throw in one skeptical mom, to boot).

Okay, so maybe Nina's having a pre-quasi-mid-life crisis. Yes, she's upset that she's not where she "should" be in life, but she's simply freaking out about it ten years sooner than everyone else. It makes sense. See, everyone else has sped past her in the life-departments of career position, marriage prospects, and — hell, even having a little spare cash in the ol' checking account. Yeah, she's a little behind. Speaking of behinds, she'll have to work on that too, if she's to start dating again.

Straightening out her life doesn't happen simply. How can it, once she's humiliated when she gets caught snared in her arch rival cousin's wedding gown at the woman's own bridal shower? (This is a good time to add that the cousin calls off the entire wedding because of Nina… long story).

Then a promotion is up for grabs at the ad agency/PR firm where Nina works as an assistant. She's got to fight for it big time and beat out the "shoo-in." Part of earning the promotion includes "babysitting" a Zsa-Zsa-Gabor-cop-slapping actress who's in town to make a comeback movie and needs help with her PR nightmare. Of course, the movie star makes Nina's life a living hell. But Nina must endure and do her job fabulously well for the next few weeks… all in time for the company's annual gala affair. It's an event where the promotion announcement will be made. An event where she must have the perfect date by her side to save face. No pressure, right?

Marathon dating doesn't come easy. See, when it comes to heartache, Nina is a bleeder, despite her lighthearted smart-alecky exterior. Her breakup with Jeremiah has left her reeling and she finds it impossible to suffer the dating scene — until she literally stumbles across DANTE. Okay, so maybe this guy hemorrhages his handsomeness all over the place. But he can usually be found straddling his motorcycle and behaving in a way indicative of a rudderless, rebel lifestyle.

Falling for Dante is as smart as running with scissors, in the dark and drunk. He's the epitome of what Nina doesn't want right now. Not with all she's trying to accomplish. But she can't help herself each time she gets sidetracked by this guy, who's all hell-bent on showing her that she's wrong in attempting to lead her life in one direction, according to convention. He feels she should fly by the seat of her panties. And Nina is torn. She's having feelings for this guy, who's feeling cool stuff for her, too. Oh, hell, why does being so bad have to feel so good?

From soup to (Dante's) nuts, the obstacles Nina faces are mounting:

(1) She's in knots trying to keep in line the aging fruitcake movie actress, especially when the woman ends up in jail. (2) She also must keep the peace with her friends. These gal-pals make matters worse for her under the guise of "just tryin' to help." With friends like these, who needs therapy? (3) She can't help but be seduced by her often polemic, but always passionate, run-ins with Dante, the stud muffin on a chopper. (4) Oh, right, then there's the evil "shoo-in" guy sabotaging her efforts for promotion at the ad agency every chance he gets. (5) Cue the ex-fiance. Now's as good a time as any to mention that Jeremiah the jockey-journalist comes back from reporting on a dangerous assignment overseas, and wants to get back together with Nina.

With Jeremiah home, Nina entertains the notion of getting back together with her repentant Geraldo-wanna-be. It would be so easy to just set her life back on its original course. After all, who knew that living life would be so much work? But she also entertains the notion that she enjoys her free-spirited romps with Dante, despite their polar-opposite views on, well, everything.

Okay, so maybe she does more than "entertain" both notions…she "entertains" both men.

The plot thickens…and so does her waistline.

Believing she "may be" a little pregnant (yeah, yeah, either you are or you aren't, unless you're in denial, then it's a definite "maybe"), Nina must make some serious choices. She needs to decide whether to tell both fathers (an egg can be dually fertilized, can't it?) about her possible pregnancy. She also must decide whom to bring to the gala since both men insist on escorting her. And, she must figure out how to get the evil "shoo-in" guy to hang himself by his own devices, revealing his incessant sabotaging in time for the gala-soiree. Finally, she must get the attention-craving movie actress to behave herself once and for all.

A couple things turn around for Nina. She comes to terms with her relationships with her mom and her friends. Then she sees a softer side to the movie actress, who's actually sympathetic to Nina's plight and a bond is formed. Nina also discovers she's not pregnant. Nevertheless, the non-birthing experience makes her grow anyway and she sees things in a new light.

She finally informs both men in her love triangle that she intends to go alone to the gala… she's learning to be happy with herself and where she is right now. She discovers that always worrying about the future has been keeping her from enjoying the present. The urgency to be where she thinks she "ought" to be in life has lessened; some things simply can't be rushed.

Does this stop the two competing men from showing up at the gala anyway? No. Both men are decked out in tuxes when they make their appearances at the affair and attempt to win her affections. She doesn't need this right now. So far, at the gala, things don't look good for her promotion. And the two men causing a testosterone-filled scene aren't helping matters.

One thing is good however, while she's juggling these two boy-toys, her previous efforts pay off in getting the evil "shoo-in" to bite himself in the ass with his rotten antics. His ploys finally backfire, getting him caught red-handed sabotaging Nina. As for Dante, well, Nina discovers he's harboring a shocking secret of his own.

Nina is ultimately offered the promotion; she accepts. But when she gets an ultimatum from both Dante and Jeremiah, telling her to choose, she asserts that she chooses neither. They must leave the gala now. Dante takes the news like a man, showing much greater chivalry and dignity than Jeremiah, who mouths off at her, spitefully revealing his true colors, and storms off.

Okay, so some parts of Nina's life are "getting there." Others, well, they ain't so good. She's lost Jeremiah again. That makes it three times now. But she's certain it will be the last, especially after she finds out why he wanted to get back together with her. Apparently, when he bagged out on their engagement, the tabloids caught wind of this and tore him to pieces for being a coward. They had a field day when they macheted his machismo in their papers and he'd become desperate to rectify his big bad rep. Imagine, going through those pains all in the name of a job…

Nina realizes Dante was right (at least to a degree) about the way she's been running her life. While she doesn't totally agree with his non-directional ways, he has helped to show her that she doesn't need to be so worked up about extreme societal convention. She knows living her life falls somewhere between the two. If only she had the chance to tell him.

She gets that chance as she leaves the gala. Dante is waiting in the shadows for her. He's sitting on his motorcycle, oozing sexuality in that suave rented tux of his. He's genuinely concerned to see if she's all right; he also wants to see if she needs a lift home.

Admittedly, she's happy Dante stuck around; it says a lot about the guy's character. She informs him how she realized that much of what he believes about life turned out to be right on the money. He corrects her, saying his beliefs were only partly true when it comes to leading your life without direction. He tells her he also came to the gala tonight to let her know something. He feels the time has come to stick around for a while and open up his dream business of a vintage motorcycle shop and touring motor club. But he wants to know one thing… does he have something worthwhile to stick around for?

She unceremoniously hikes up her sequin gala gown, straddles the back of his motorcycle, and wraps her arms around his waist. "Hell if I know," she answers happily, "but for now, let's just ride."

SUCCESSFUL SYNOPSIS: MYSTERY NOVEL

(E-mail version)

SWIFT JUSTICE

By Laura DaSilverio

Synopsis

When CHARLOTTE "CHARLIE" SWIFT, former Air Force investigator turned barely solvent PI, confronts an armed woman in her office first thing Monday morning, she knows the week is going to suck. And when she finds out she must accept the woman, GIGI GOLDMAN, as her partner in Swift Investigations, she hatches a plan to get rid of Gigi. (LES GOLDMAN, Gigi's husband and Charlie's silent — emphasis on silent —partner, embezzled funds from his businesses and decamped to Costa Rica with his personal trainer, leaving Gigi nothing but the house, the Hummer, and half-interest in Swift Investigations.) A pampered socialite in her fifties, Gigi doesn't strike Charlie as investigator material and she resolves to "persuade" the woman to give up on PI work by assigning her all the most tedious and grubby tasks.

Meanwhile, a client turns up with a missing person case that challenges even Charlie's investigative skills. MELISSA LLOYD found a baby on her doorstep with a note asking her to take care of it for a few days. Not unnaturally, in Charlie's opinion, she wants to find the mother who, Melissa confesses, is her daughter. Piece of cake, Charlie thinks, until she asks for the daughter's name and description, only to hear that Melissa doesn't know because she's never met her. Huh? Turns out, Melissa got pregnant as a teen and gave the baby girl up for adoption. Apparently, the now sixteen-year-old has located Melissa and ditched her own infant on the doorstep. Find the teen and give the baby back, Melissa orders Charlie.

Following clues culled from the one-of-a-kind blanket BABY OLIVIA came swaddled in, Charlie sallies forth from Colorado Springs to interview a goat herder/artist in Larkspur and a wine shop owner in Denver. Her queries net her the name of the girl who left the baby with Melissa and she heads home triumphantly, only to learn from a police detective buddy, that the body of a Jane Doe fits the description of Charlie's missing teen. Charlie e-mails the detective the photos she got in Denver and receives confirmation that the dead girl is ELIZABETH SPROUSE, Melissa Lloyd's daughter, Olivia's mother, and the city's twenty-seventh homicide of the year. When Charlie breaks the news to her client and shows her the photos, Melissa faints. Revived, she tells Charlie she knows the girl in the photos. Calling herself Beth, and saying her husband was a soldier deployed in Iraq, the girl has done piece-work sewing for Melissa's interior design business for the better part of a year.

Charlie figures she's done her job by locating Olivia's mother, but Melissa changes her assignment: find the baby's father and offload Olivia on him. This task proves much harder as Charlie delves into Elizabeth's life, talking to her high school counselor, her best friend, and the parents who adopted her as an infant. The father is a pastor in the style of an Old Testament prophet and the mother is a cowed homemaker. When Elizabeth ran away, her father was plotting an arranged marriage for her with a 45-year-old member of his congregation with the money and connections to get Pastor Sprouse his own

TV show. The alleged fiancé, Seth Johnson, an immensely rich and politically powerful rancher, vehemently denies having sex with Elizabeth and threatens Charlie with un-named consequences if she investigates him further. In fact, no one Charlie talks to can point to a potential father for Olivia. All of them, however, agree Elizabeth was obsessed with finding her birth mother. Charlie locates the PI Elizabeth hired to find her mother and the PI says the girl seemed a little "off" in her motives. She wasn't looking for a joyful Hallmark reunion, the PI opines.

As Charlie's frustration mounts, she must deal with the results of Gigi's catastrophic attempts at investigation, including burning down the organic fast food joint where she was undercover as the mascot, Bernie the Bison, and blowing up a meth lab during the botched surveillance of an alleged adulterer. Each time, she manages to solve the case and generate positive publicity for Swift Investigations. Exasperated by the woman's refusal to quit (despite a broken arm), Charlie gives Gigi summons work to do and continues unraveling Elizabeth's surprisingly complex life.

Charlie thinks she's making progress when she discovers Elizabeth was trolling surrogate mother sites on the internet. Olivia's father must be STEPHAN FALSTOW, Charlie decides, the male half of a couple Elizabeth met via a surrogacy site. Interviewing Mrs. Falstow dashes that theory: Elizabeth was already pregnant when she met the Falstow. They agreed to pay her expenses in return for permission to adopt Olivia. JACQUELINE FALSTOW, desperate for a baby, has longed to know the baby's fate since learning of Elizabeth's death. Suspecting Charlie knows where the baby is, she follows her to a meeting with DETECTIVE MONTGOMERY (who threatens to arrest Charlie for second-degree kidnapping if she doesn't reveal the baby's location) and then almost to Melissa Lloyd's front door. Charlie, realizing she's being followed, traps Mrs. Falstow in a cul de sac and confronts her. Charlie, annoyed with herself for almost leading Falstow to the baby, continues to the Lloyd house and meets IAN LLOYD, Melissa's husband. He'd run into Elizabeth only a couple of times and still doesn't realize that Olivia is Melissa's grand-daughter. He's never wanted children, however, and is eager to see the last of Olivia. (He thinks Melissa is taking care of her for a friend).

An urgent phone call draws Charlie away from the Lloyds and by the time she's finished persuading the Pine Creek Golf Course manager not to press charges against Gigi for drowning a cart while trying to serve a summons, Melissa Lloyd has fired her. Why, Charlie asks? She sees past Melissa's concocted explanation and realizes the woman loves Olivia and wants to keep her. She's confessed the truth to her husband and is no longer interested in locating the baby's father. Accepting her fee and driving back to the office, Charlie ponders the women who desperately want Olivia — Janet Falstow, Elizabeth's adopted mother, and Melissa Lloyd — and the men who could, conceivably, have fathered the baby: Stefan Falstow (who knew Elizabeth earlier than his wife suspected), PASTOR SPROUSE (who several people suspect of abusing his step-daughter), the high-school counselor, the lawyer who runs a shady practice introducing pregnant teens to rich parents desperate enough to buy babies, or SETH JOHNSON (with three failed marriages behind him and an obsession with producing an heir). To stop Charlie's investigation of his affairs, Johnson threatens to put her out of business by buying out her partner (Gigi) and buying up her mortgage and foreclosing at the first opportunity. Charlie must, against all her instincts, beg Gigi to stay on as her partner and not sell out. The women take the first tentative steps toward friendship.

Just as Charlie reaches her office, trying to come to terms with not being able to close the case, Melissa calls. Olivia has been kidnapped! Charlie immediately calls Detective Montgomery and, convinced she knows who has kidnapped the baby, heads to the Falstow house with Gigi. It soon becomes obvious Janet Falstow did not take the baby. As Charlie's sifting through all the data she amassed during the investigation, Montgomery calls to say Melissa denies a kidnapping took place. The police suspect she's lying and Montgomery wants Charlie to talk to her. On the way to the Lloyd house, the pieces fall into place for Charlie and she calls Melissa to ask where Ian is. Melissa initially refuses to believe her husband could have taken the baby, but agrees to activate his truck's anti-theft GPS tracker.

Charlie and Gigi locate Ian and Olivia at a Walmart south of Colorado Springs. (He stopped to purchase a car seat and diapers, not having planned his kidnapping very well.) He wasn't going to hurt the baby, he assures them when they trap him; he was going to take her across state lines and leave her at a fire station or hospital. Once Melissa told him Olivia was Elizabeth's baby, he knew her DNA could connect him to Elizabeth and her death. Her accidental death, he hastens to add. When Elizabeth birthed Olivia and decided to keep the baby, she needed money to get away from Colorado and the sure-to-be-furious Falstows. She called Ian and threatened to tell Melissa about their brief affair if he didn't help her financially. He met her at a secluded location, planning to persuade her, he says, to give up the baby. But she didn't have the baby with her (having dropped it off at Melissa's). Elizabeth shocks him by saying she plotted their affair as revenge against Melissa for abandoning her. She'd tracked her birth mother down, with nebulous ideas for revenge that crystallized when she met Ian.

What better revenge than to sleep with Melissa's husband? Appalled, he punches Elizabeth and she falls, breaking her neck on his F-150 bumper

Knowing the police are on their way to the Walmart, Ian tries to escape. Sprinting to the back of the store, he hijacks a Fluffy-Wip truck from the loading dock, with Charlie in hot pursuit on foot. Gigi appears in the Hummer and Ian wrecks the truck to avoid a collision. Whipped cream oozes into the parking lot and customers frolic in it as the police arrive to take him into custody.

In the end of SWIFT JUSTICE, the 80,000-word first in a PI mystery series, Melissa ends up with the baby while Ian awaits trial. Charlie and Gigi capitalize on the publicity generated by the successful case and move forward to their next case as partners.

SUCCESSFUL SYNOPSIS: YOUNG ADULT NOVEL

(E-mail version)

REVOLUTION, SIZE SMALL

By Loretta Nyhan

Synopsis

Sixteen-year-old TRUDIE MORESCO is increasingly unhappy living in the shadows of her larger than life parents: FIONA, a local celeb known for her eco-activism, and TONY, an adrenaline addict serving Doctors in Crisis in Africa. She experiments with ways to create an identity separate from that of her parents, mainly, exploring her interest in photography and flirting with EMIL, a recent immigrant and Fiona's intern. Emil likes Trudie, but stops the romance before anything serious happens: He's still getting over someone from back home. Someone who, as Trudie later learns, happens to be a boy.

After a night of drinking, Trudie's growing frustration culminates in a really dumb decision. She breaks into the property of CLINTER FLETCHER, a real estate developer intent on ruining her mom's plans for a community garden, and etches her feelings onto his Lincoln Navigator with her Swiss Army knife. Luckily, the Gross Hills Police Department has a program for "good kids who do stupid things." Instead of standing in front of a judge, Trudie can work off her debt to society by working for Mr. Fletcher, painting one of his investment properties.

On the first day of her prison sentence Trudie is not met by Mr. Fletcher, but by CONNOR, his troubled stepson, and Trudie's ideological opposite. Surprisingly they work well together, and as a tentative friendship develops, Connor gives Trudie glimpses into the lives of the secretive Fletchers. Her friends think Trudie's stumbled into the perfect opportunity to spy on behalf of her mother's activist group. Trudie agrees but becomes conflicted when she senses Connor likes her in the way she wishes Emil would.

As Trudie spends less time with her friends and more with Connor, his roundabout stabs at asking her out develop a certain appeal and she agrees to have dinner at his house. Afterwards, Connor offers Trudie some information Fiona could use to fight Clint's bid on the community land. Though the evidence is pretty circumstantial, alerting the zoning board would assure a win for Fiona, and destroy Clint's ability to build anywhere in Gross Hills.

Trudie struggles with what to do. After watching her mom tirelessly lead the community on the two-year garden campaign, failure would be devastating, but might also bring her father home from Africa. Connor seems to have a score to settle with his stepdad, making Trudie feel like a convenient way to get the job done. She needs help, but has fallen away from the people who could best offer it. Fiona is distracted and silently grieving for a marriage put on hold; Trudie's best friend nurses hurt feelings after Trudie refused to share the details of her relationship with Emil, and Tony's communication with her practically consists of one-line e-mails and a link to his Facebook page. Trudie shares her information with the person of last resort, who refuses to tell her what to do, and instead advises Trudie to do what she feels is right.

Trudie attends the board meeting, with a manila envelope as her contribution to the hearing. After the board decides in Fiona's favor, a member of the committee hands the folder to Fiona, telling her the contents really showed the committee the garden's potential. Fiona opens it and finds a handbound album of photos depicting herbs from her garden: dill bursting like fireworks on the Fourth of July, lavender swaying in the breeze, soft and hazy chamomile, and, finally, a mint plant Trudie shot with her 1968 Pentax on a day Emil left her alone on the contested patch of land to think.

To celebrate the win, the group heads back to Trudie's house for a party. As people set up tables and light candles in the garden, Trudie feels a little overwhelmed and heads up to her room for a breather.

She enters her darkened room to find Tony sitting on her bed, twenty pounds thinner, with knobby knees and stories to tell. They head down to the party, and while Tony and Fiona get to the business of working out their relationship, Trudie does the same with both Emil and Connor. Nothing is completely settled, but as Trudie has learned, when presented with an either/or decision, it's perfectly appropriate to make your choice from the small space between the two. She realizes this as she takes Connor's hand and they join the party, together.

Sample Formatted Manuscript Pages

TITLE PAGE

B. Hudson
1234 Main Street
Anywhere, USA 11111
(555) 555-5555
author@myemail.com

80,000 words

THE PATH

A Novel

by B. Hudson

TABLE OF CONTENTS PAGE

Hudson/THE PATH/Contents

Table Of Contents

Chapter 1: Observations at the Saloon 1

Chapter 2: Rogues Ride Again 25

Chapter 3: On the Road to Las Cruces 47

Chapter 4: Gunslinger 73

Chapter 5: The Body 90

Chapter 6: Desert Silence 122

FIRST PAGE OF CHAPTER FORMAT

Hudson / THE PATH   *1*

CHAPTER 1
OBSERVATIONS AT THE SALOON

I know it must sound callous, but Billy McGinty looked like a repulsive little freak. I could hardly believe my eyes when I first saw him. Like a human crab he shuffled into Bob's Place, an old-fashioned oak-paneled saloon where I had just taken shelter from the rain. He barely stood four feet, with an enormous chest borne by skinny, bandy legs. The span of that chest would not have disgraced a man twice his size, but it made him look ridiculous and indeed somewhat sinister, as I said, like a crab. His head, topped by a shock of black hair, was of normal size but his forehead was so excessively large that it dwarfed the features below it.

A black fringe of meeting eyebrows shaded his small cavernous eyes. His nose was short and fleshy with wide nostrils that bristled with hairs. A straight, thin-lipped mouth and a pointed chin completed his repellent face that was always darkened by a 5 o'clock shadow. He really was a walking nightmare, an ogre from Dickensian slums, a kind of Neanderthal man who nevertheless had a touch of melancholy about him.

I often saw him before we really got to know each other. We had

FORMATTING FOR SUBSEQUENT CHAPTER PAGES

Hudson / THE PATH   **5**

Billy rose. Faster than a jumping spider he pounced on the first one and before the bully could even move he had suffered a barrage of thudding blows in the stomach that made him double up and crash to the floor, dragging along his friend with barstools and all. Billy's immediate victim was out, but his mate struggled to his feet, towering above Billy like King Kong. He uttered a snarling curse and clenched his meaty fists. But again Billy demonstrated his uncanny powers.

He took a flying leap, sort of climbed into the man, and dealt him such a blow on the nose that it cracked and spurted blood. Dropping back on his feet, Billy grabbed a stool, swung it like a base-ball bat and brought it down with crushing force on the head of his opponent who, already dazed, toppled like a tree. Without paying any further attention to his victims, Billy ambled back to the stool beside mine, climbed on to it, and shot me a fierce, questioning glance, as if he were looking for an excuse to knock me out as well.

"Good show," I said, to humor him.

He seemed to like that and grinned, revealing a hole where his front teeth should have been.

"Muscle," he said. "Arms of steel, mine are."

"Remarkable," I said.

He froze at once.

"What do you mean, remarkable? For a dwarf?"

Successful Book Proposal

SAMPLE PROPOSAL

A Proposal for

Modern Traditions:
Inspiring Ideas for Incorporating Yesterday's
Customs into Today's Wedding

by Gina Cunningham

1234 Main Street
Anywhere USA
(555) 555-5555
name@myemail.com

Table of Contents

Introduction

Overview 1

Markets3

Spin-offs 4

Promotion 4

Competitive & Complementary Books 7

About the Author 9

The Outline

    Chapter Summary 10

Sample Chapter

    Chapter 7: The Ceremony 12

Supplemental Material

    Press Clippings Featuring the Author XX

INTRODUCTION

Overview

Engaged couples want weddings that blend tradition and personal style. They are looking to the past for inspiring ways to transform a modern wedding into a meaningful experience.

Modern Traditions will be the first book to present traditional cultural wedding elements with a twist; updated and reinterpreted for today's couple. The book will outline cultural customs, rituals, and symbolism from around the world associated with music, dance, food, ceremony, design, and decor and provide inspiring ideas for readers to adapt traditions to their wedding.

Modern Traditions will help brides and grooms design a signature wedding that reflects their style as a couple by defining ways to honor their heritage, adopt a custom, update a tradition, or create a new ritual to personalize their wedding and pay elegant tribute to what is meaningful to them.

Industry publications and professionals note the trend toward incorporating, updating, and "borrowing" wedding traditions. Bride's magazine reports, "couples are choosing to observe centuries-old traditions, updating them to reflect their own personalities. And more couples than ever before are including ethnic customs from their heritages in wedding celebrations." *Modern Bride* magazine observes in their 2002 report, "couples are borrowing traditions from their own heritage or other cultures [for their wedding]." Bridal Guide writes, "Many couples select traditions from a variety of cultures because the idea resonates with them. They like the symbolism behind these acts and incorporate them [into their wedding], regardless of the heritage." The book will provide a much-needed resource in the fast growing wedding design market. Modern Traditions will appeal to:

- Couples wanting to incorporate aspects of each other's culture into the wedding

- Couples looking for a guide to provide practical and stylish ideas for incorporating traditional elements into the wedding

- Couples looking for ideas to personalize their wedding

- Couples wanting to add meaningful elements to their wedding

- Couples wanting to differentiate their wedding from others and create a unique celebration

- Wedding coordinators, designers, event planners, and catering managers looking for new ideas and inspiration

As a wedding coordinator and designer, the author has planned numerous celebrations incorporating her clients' cultures and personalities. From Irish handfastings to African-American ribbon tying, the author creates inspiring events for couples. The author will present ideas from her diverse portfolio and create new designs gathered from extensive cultural research.

Vibrant photographs of design elements, sidebars with real couples' stories, references to celebrities' wedding designs, checklists outlining updated ideas, and a complete resource list will add value and visual appeal.

The finished manuscript will contain 250 pages, including twenty pages of back matter, seventy-three photographs, and nineteen black and white photographs, and one chart. The book will be divided into three sections: ceremony, design, and celebration, with eighteen chapters, five design element inserts, and ten couples' stories. The manuscript will be completed six months after the book advance is received.

The author will ask the following authorities to write an introduction or cover quote:

- Colin Cowie, celebrity wedding designer, author, and television host

- Maria Melinger-McBride, wedding designer, author of *The Perfect Wedding* and *The Perfect Wedding Reception*, contributing editor for *Bride's* magazine

- Vera Wang, celebrity wedding fashion designer and author

- Carley Roney, author *The Knot Guide to Wedding Traditions and Vows*, creator TheKnot.com

Back matter will include a resource list, a chart of traditions by culture, recommended reading, author's biography, and a form for the readers to note their design ideas, photo credits, a feedback request form, and index.

Markets

More than 2.4 million couples marry each year in the United States according to *Modern Bride*. The Great Bridal Expo reports that weddings are a $92 billion per year industry. Gerard Monaghan, president of the Association of Bridal Consultants, adds that wedding inquiries are up 25% since September 11, 2001 and states, "[according to a survey of 2,600 professional wedding coordinators] there is a growing demand for weddings celebrating heritage."

According to the Great Bridal Expo, wedding customers are 90% female, age 25-34, college graduates, with an average combined income level of $75,000. Engaged consumers are recession proof, constantly renewing, and have high immediate needs. Couples purchase wedding items at bridal fairs, wedding salons, event showrooms, and stationary stores, and via the internet. A bride spends over 100 hours designing the wedding. Brides turn to design books, wedding experts, bridal magazines, and television shows for inspiration.

Markets for the book include engaged couples and members of the hospitality industry: wedding designers, coordinators, and venue catering managers.

Spin-offs

Modern Traditions will be the first in a series of six wedding design books including:

- *A Heritage Wedding: Culturally Inspired Designs to Personalize Your Wedding*

- *Elegant Themes: Stylish Designs to Personalize Your Wedding*

- *Defining Your Wedding Style: How To Reveal Your Personality to Design a Unique Celebration*

- *Inspired Ideas for Designing an Elegant Wedding on a Minimal Budget*

- *Stylish Ideas for Designing a Destination Wedding*

Promotion

The author will do the following to help the publisher promote the book:

Publicity Campaign

Expand the author's current publicity campaign by hiring a public relations firm with expertise in book promotion to obtain national television interviews and magazine and newspaper features.

Media Kit & Video

Expand the author's current media kit. Press kit will include the author's biography, headshot, book cover jacket (galley), author Q&A sheet, Rolodex card, book reviews, and press clippings. Author will hire award-winning videography company Blvd. Video Productions to produce an 8-minute video featuring author interviews and wedding design highlights. Produce 1,000 Rolodex cards with "wedding expert" headline to be sent to media and journalists. Author will commission Century Guild Press to create a letterpress media box to hold the press kit, video, and tie-in promotional items. Author will make press kit and her media contact list available to the publisher.

Send Books to Opinion-Makers

If publisher supplies copies of the books, the author will mail twenty-five books to leading wedding industry opinion-makers.

Author Magazine Articles and Column

Pitch author-written feature articles to media contacts at national wedding magazines including *Martha Stewart Weddings, Bridal Guide, Modern Bride, Conde Nast's Brides,* and *Elegant Bride.* Pitch a "Modern Traditions" column to *Elegant Bride Magazine.*

Television Special

Approach production company contacts to produce a television special based on Modern Traditions. With the author's association with Lifetime Television, the network would be a good placement for the show.

Obtain Appearances on Design Shows and Wedding Shows

Contact design and wedding shows to be a featured expert. Shows include: Martha Stewart Living (CBS), You're Invited (Style Network), Weddings of a Lifetime (Lifetime Television), InStyle Wedding Special (NBC), and other current wedding shows in production.

Bridal Fairs

Author will provide 20,000 book postcards (with book cover and purchase information) to The Great Bridal Expo. The postcards will be used as "bag stuffers" and handed to attendees at eighteen national bridal fairs located in: Philadelphia, New York City, Washington D.C., Baltimore, Long Island, Boston, Detroit, Dallas, Miami, Atlanta, Fort Lauderdale, San Francisco, Anaheim, Los Angeles, Denver, Phoenix, Cleveland, and Cincinnati. Author will give The Great Bridal Expo thirty-six copies (two copies per city) of Modern Traditions to be given as prizes to attendees. Author will conduct "Modern Traditions" workshops at select bridal shows.

Wedding and Event Industry Conferences

Author will attend, speak, and sell books at the four leading wedding and event industry conferences each year: The Special Event (sponsored by the International Special Events Society), The Business of Brides (sponsored by the Association of Bridal Consultants), Event Solutions, and the National Association of Catering Executives.

Web site

Expand the author's current Web site to include an updated author appearance schedule for television and magazine features, creative wedding ideas and tips, links to bookseller's Web site to purchase the book, author's biography, press page (for media to contact the author), resources for purchasing wedding items associated with the book, and a monthly contest to win a one-hour telephone consultation with the author. Promote the book online with "live chats" or interviews with AOL's writer's club, **Amazon.com** writer interviews, **barnesandnoble.com**, **theknot.com**, **weddingchannel.com**, **modernbride.com**, and Martha Stewart Weddings online.

Competitive Books

There are no competitive books currently on the market that explore cultural customs and provide updated interpretations and ideas for incorporating them into the wedding design. The books that would most closely compete with Modern Traditions are:

The *Knot Guide to Wedding Vows and Traditions: Readings, Rituals, Music, Dance, Speeches, and Toasts* by Carley Roney, Broadway Books, 2000, paperback, 200 pages, $15.00. A bestseller in Theknot.com series. Provides cultural and religious wedding suggestions. Book does not provide design ideas or update traditions. Topics are limited to wedding readings, toasts, speeches, ceremony vows, and music selection.

A Bride's Book of Wedding Traditions: A Treasury of Ideas for Making Your Wedding The Most Memorable Day Ever by Arlene Hamilton Stewart, Hearst Books, 1995, 4 printings, hardcover, 300 pages, $18.00. Details the history of marriage and the origins of wedding custom. Only covers English and American traditions. Provides only a few design ideas. No photos.

Timeless Traditions: A Couple's Guide to Wedding Customs Around the World by Lisl M. Spangenberg, Universe, 2001, paperback, 232 pages, $22.50. An extensive, though not exhaustive, collection of cultural wedding traditions, sorted by country. Customs and traditions are outdated and impractical. Author does not provide design ideas or suggestions for updating customs for the modern bride. No photos.

Complementary Books

Wedding Rites: The Complete Guide to Traditional Weddings by Michael P. Foley, St. Augustine Press, 2002, hardcover, 256 pages, $35.00. Book provides a comprehensive collection of wedding music, readings, vows, prayers, ceremonies, and blessings from various religions around the world. Religious customs compliment Modern Traditions cultural customs.

Complementary Books by Publisher:

Wedding design, wedding planning, and wedding etiquette books are good companions to Modern Traditions.

Chronicle Books: *The Anti-Bride Guide* by Carolyn Gerin, *Wedding Showers* by Michele Adams, *The Wedding Planner* by Genevieve Morgan, *Weddings for Grownups* by Caroll Stoner.

Crown Books: *Martha Stewart's Wedding Planner* by Martha Stewart, *Priceless Weddings* by Kathleen Kennedy, *Bride's Wedding Book* by Elizabeth Hilliard.

Adams Media Corporation: *The Everything Wedding Book* (series), *Loving Vows* by Barbara Eklof, *The Creative Wedding Idea Book* by Jaqueline Smith.

Sterling Publishing: *Wedding Flowers* by Iain Thomson, *Wedding Decorations on a Budget* by Jo Packman, *Wedding Toasts and Vows* by Bette Matthews, *Wedding Style* by Sy Snarr.

HarperCollins Publishing: *The Perfect Wedding Reception* by Maria Melinger-McBride, *The Perfect Wedding* by Maria Melinger-McBride, *Wedding Details* by Mary Norden, *Legendary Brides* by Letitia Baldridge, *How to "I Do"* by Holly Lefevre, *Emily Post's Weddings* by Peggy Post.

Berkeley Publishing Group: *Words for the Wedding* by Wendy Paris, *The Wedding Guide for the Grownup Bride* by Shelley Christiansen, *The Wedding Wise Planner* by Suzanne Kresse.

Hearst Books: *Town and Country Elegant Weddings* by Stacey Okun, *A Romantic Wedding Planner* by Victoria Magazine, *Creating a Beautiful Wedding* by Victoria Magazine.

Random House, Inc.: *With This Ring* by Joanna Weaver, *This is Your Day* by Lisa Weiss, *Real Weddings* by Sally Kilbridge.

Michael Friedman Publishing Group, Inc.: *Centerpieces and Table Accents* by Kathy Passero, *A Wedding Workbook* by Bette Matthews, *Cakes* by Bette Matthews, *For Your Wedding* (series).

Steart, Tabori & Chang, Inc.: *Bouquets: A Year of Flowers for the Bride* by Marsha Heckman, *The Perfect Wedding Cake* by Kate Manchester, *A Perfect Home Wedding* by Kerry Eielson.

About the Author

As a celebrated wedding designer, coordinator, and owner of Wedding Design Studio in Los Angeles, I create and produce distinctive weddings for couples. My diverse portfolio includes both celebrity couples (actors and prominent sports figures) and everyday couples. I have been featured on several episodes of Lifetime Television's "Weddings of a Lifetime", The Today Show, and Good Morning, America. I author a bi-monthly column on theme weddings in *Inside Weddings Magazine* and speak to more than 50,000 event professionals at conferences each year. My blog, Designing Poetic Weddings, receives over 5,000 hits per day and I have a database of 85,000 subscribers for my monthly e-newsletter. I have been featured in *Elegant Bride Magazine, Bridal Guide, Conde' Nast Bride's WeddingBells, The Knot WeddingPages, InStyle Magazine, Martha Stewart Weddings,* and *The Los Angeles Times.*

THE OUTLINE

Chapter List

Acknowledgements

Introduction

Chapter 1: Getting Accustomed

SECTION ONE: CEREMONY

Chapter 2:   Custom Tailored — Wedding Attire, Rings, and Accessories

Chapter 3:   When December Snows Fall Fast — Wedding Location, Date and Time

Insert 1:   The Ties That Bind — Wedding Knots

Chapter 4:   Embracing the Sun — Rites of Passage and Pre-Wedding Celebrations

Chapter 5:   Quill and Ink — Invitations and Programs

Insert 2:   To Speak of Love — Poetry, Quotes, and Readings

Chapter 6:   Angels on Horseback — Wedding Transportation

Chapter 7:   Ceremonia — The Ceremony Elements

SECTION TWO: DÉCOR AND DESIGN

Chapter 8:   Walking Among The Stones – Ceremony Décor

Chapter 9:   Lavender and Edelweiss — Bouquets & Boutonnieres

Chapter 10:   Of Branches and Ivy — Wreaths and Garlands

Insert 3:   Illumination — Candles and Fire

Chapter 11:   Cattails and Harvest Wheat — Setting the Table

Chapter 12:   Of Heaven and Earth — Design Details

Insert 4:   A Sweet Life — Honey

Chapter 13:   Red Boxes and Wishing Stones — Gifts, Favors, and Keepsakes

SECTION THREE — CELEBRATION

Chapter 14:   Fiddlers, Pipers, and Ragamuffins — Music, Dance, and Entertainment

Chapter 15:   Wild Berries and Whiskey — Food and Wine

Chapter 16:   To Taste Abundance — The Cake

Insert 5:   Rosemary for Remembrance — Herbs

Chapter 17:   Dancing on the Embers — Reception Customs

Chapter 18:   Bringing Your Wedding Vision to Life

Design Forms

Resources

Recommended Reading

Chart of Customs by Culture

Index

About the Author

Send Suggestions Page

SECTION ONE — CEREMONY

Chapter 1: Getting Accustomed

The first chapter discusses why couples include traditions in their weddings, then goes on to give readers an understanding of how to incorporate traditions into the wedding. It outlines universal elements and provides options for honoring one's culture, updating traditions, blending cultures and traditions, borrowing traditions, and creating new traditions. The chapter explains the importance of intent in creating new rituals and gives "how-to's" for getting started, finding inspiration, selecting items, and designing the flow of elements to run smoothly. The author provides specific ideas for sharing the significance of the traditions with the wedding guests. The chapter concludes by encouraging readers to explore and identify what is important to them as a couple.

Chapter 2: Custom Tailored: Wedding Attire, Rings, and Accessories

Chapter two outlines traditional wedding attire, accessories, and rings by culture and provides stylish ideas for incorporating and updating elements. The chapter begins with wedding clothes: dresses (colors, style, embroidery, symbolism, fabrics, and patterns), heirloom gowns, groom's attire, wedding attendant's clothes, and shoes; and then discusses hairstyles, special tokens, veils and headpieces, accessories, handkerchiefs, and ribbons. A section on rings: types of rings (including Claddagh, Gimmal, posie, Celtic, Luckenboot, crested, gemstones, precious stones, birthstones, keeper rings, regard rings, and Fede rings), engraving rings, and meanings associated with rings completes the chapter. "A Couple's Story" features Melissa and David: A Wedding with English, Asian, African-American, Israeli, and Celtic elements.

Chapter 3: When December Snow Falls Fast: Wedding Location, Date, and Time

In Victorian times, falling snow on a couple's wedding day was believed to signify a happy marriage. "When December's snow falls fast, Marry, and true love will last" — Old English folk rhyme.

The chapter outlines traditional wedding sites and selection of the wedding date and time. Traditions are listed by culture; ideas are provided for incorporating and updating them. Items included in the chapter are: outdoor weddings, historical venues, sacred places, divination techniques using fortune-tellers and astrologers, benefits of seasonal wedding celebrations, and preferred days and time. "A Couple's Story" features Jennifer and Lee: A Wedding with Filipino and Irish Elements and a beach theme.

Special Insert 1: The Ties That Bind: Wedding Knots

Knots are one of the oldest and universal wedding elements. The special insert elaborates on numerous ways to creatively incorporate knots into the wedding. Highlights include: harvest knots, ribbon knots, bouquet knots, cookie knots, wrist knots, and handfasting knots.

Chapter 4: Embracing the Sun: Rites of Passage and Pre-Wedding Celebrations

On the morning of her wedding a Native-American bride greets the sun in a ritual representing her passage into a new life.

The chapter explores the universal practice of purification and transformation rituals, and provides ways to incorporate and update elements for the modern bride and groom. Highlights include henna and body painting, beauty applications, cleansing and symbolic baths, fragrant massages, wedding eve dinners, wedding showers, bachelor and bachelorette parties, engagement parties, and spiritual preparation ceremonies. "A Couple's Story" features Moira and Andrew: A Wedding with Native-American and French elements.

Chapter 5: Quill and Ink: Invitations and Programs

With quill and ink, medieval monks inscribed the first paper invitations in calligraphy.

The chapter showcases invitation customs by culture, ways to elegantly update them, and the inclusion of cultural traditions. The chapter proposes ancient design options: engraving, calligraphy, letterpress, oral biddings, heraldry, coats of arms, emblems, and artwork; then moves on to items included in an invitation and program: myths, legends, family stories, photos and renderings, gifts and tokens, and the symbolism and significance of selected elements. The chapter closes by emphasizing the visual importance the invitation and program have on the wedding.

Insert 2: To Speak of Love: Poetry, Quotes, and Readings

The special insert focuses on how to use poetry, quotes, and readings throughout the wedding design: invitations, programs, place cards, favors, toasts, and the ceremony.

Chapter 6: Angeles on Horseback: Wedding Transportation

A Corsican bride rides a white horse to her wedding ceremony. Along the way, she launches an olive branch down a stream to signify the abundance, peace, and happiness that will flow through her marriage.

The chapter will list traditional, unique ways couples, and their guests, are transported to the wedding: horses, carriages, sleighs, foot, and specialty vehicles.

Chapter 7: Ceremonial: The Ceremony Elements

The chapter identifies cultural ceremony elements and suggests ways to update, borrow, and personalize them to create a meaningful and memorable event. The chapter begins with the bridal path, processional, and fire rituals, then details ceremony exchanges, sharing rituals, bindings and handfastings, offerings, and acceptance practices. The chapter concludes with unification ceremonies, rituals for honoring the family, symbolic tosses, and the recessional. "A Couple's Story" features Rebekah and Brooks: A Wedding with Celtic and Medieval elements.

SECTION TWO: DÉCOR AND DESIGN

Chapter 8: Walking Among The Stones: Ceremony Décor

Stones have long been associated with wedding ceremonies and incorporated into the décor. To show her acceptance of the groom and commitment to the marriage, an Apache bride walks along a path of stones.

The chapter outlines traditional ceremony décor by culture and offers ways to create new designs. Starting with the creation of the altar, the chapter then moves on to canopies, banners, circles, stones, and the aisle. Recommendations for ceremony gifts and guest participation are included.

Chapter 9: Lavender and Edelweiss: Bouquets and Boutonnieres

Boutonnieres are a legacy from medieval times when a knight would wear a flower or other item to match his lady's' colors.

The traditional use and origin of bouquets and boutonnieres is discussed. A thorough list of flowers and herbs is presented by culture, country of origin, season, color, and associated meanings and symbolism. "A Couple's Story" features Monica and Bernd: A Wedding with German, Southern, and African-American elements.

Chapter 10: Of Branches and Ivy: Wreaths and Garlands

Wedding wreaths symbolize the circle of life. Ivy, representing fidelity, happiness, and marriage, and branches considered life's essence, are commonly incorporated into the floral design.

Chapter ten builds on chapter nine; elaborating on flowers and herbs used in wreaths and garlands. Hair wreaths, door wreaths, plant talismans, and necklace garlands are discussed.

Insert 3: Illumination: Candles and Fire

The special insert looks at the traditional, universal use of fire in wedding rituals and offers suggestions for bringing it into today's celebrations. Candlelit ceremonies, favors, and centerpieces are presented along with new traditions and ideas.

Chapter 11: Cattails and Harvest Wheat: Setting the Table

Traditionally, wedding celebrations were often held during autumn, after the harvest. Cattails and sheaves of wheat, seasonal items, and fertility symbols were frequent décor elements.

The décor of the table is the focus of chapter eleven. First, table styles, sizes, and room placement are examined, followed by a presentation of fabric treatments, linens, and napkins. Next, we look at centerpieces, dishware, and glasses. An investigation of table display items completes the chapter. "A Couple's Story" features Yu Mei and Jeffrey: A Wedding with Chinese and Latin elements.

Chapter 12: Of Heaven and Earth: Design Details

Asian weddings abound with myth, symbolism, and balance: yin and yang, mirth and harmony, and heaven and earth — represented in the wedding décor by white paper tablets.

The chapter elaborates on the design details: furnishings, lighting, and artistic elements. Colors, their meanings, and significance, are examined by culture. Cultural symbols — butterflies, feathers, and maypoles — are explored for inspiration and creativity. Designing place cards, using ribbons, and displaying hope chests round out the chapter.

Insert 4: A Sweet Life: Honey

Another common wedding element, honey, is investigated in the special insert. Suggestions for bringing honey into your wedding in a playful and poignant way are provided. Ceremony tastings, décor, favors, and menu items are included.

Chapter 13: Red Boxes and Wishing Stones: Gifts, Favors, and Keepsakes

In an old Celtic tradition, guests throw pebbles into a river near the ceremony site, while making a wish for the couple. An updated version of this time-honored ritual will create a beautiful keepsake for the bride and groom: at the ceremony location, have guests place small stones, along with their wishes, in a glass container filled with water that you can keep in your new home.

The chapter identifies traditional gifts and favors for guests, by country, provides inspiring suggestions for including unique items, and expands on ways to create meaningful keepsakes. Guest writings, family ties, and charitable contributions are covered, along with dozens of distinctive ideas. "A Couple's Story" features Sumi and Matt: A Wedding with Indian and European elements.

SECTION THREE: CELEBRATION

Chapter 14: Fiddlers, Pipers, and Ragamuffins: Music, Dance, and Entertainment

In a rural Irish custom, it is considered a sign of good luck if strawboys or ragamuffins "attend" the cerebration and dance with the bride.

The chapter explores music, dance, and entertainment associated with each culture. Instrumentation, guest participation, and the hiring of entertainers are discussed. A comprehensive list of music and dances is included. "A Couple's Story" features Adrienne and Bud: A Wedding with Scottish and Hawaiian elements.

Chapter 15: Wild Berries and Whiskey: Food and Wine

Honor your heritage, include a favorite beverage, or create a unique twist on an age-old cultural item by providing whiskey shots (a traditional celebratory drink of Ireland and Scotland) during the cocktail hour or as a champagne substitute in the ritual wedding toast.

The chapter outlines traditional drinks, wedding food, and dining customs by culture. The chapter begins with selecting the right type of meal service for your wedding: brunch, tea, breakfast, cocktails, dinner, or buffet and then expands on the ideas for the cocktail hour, lists sample menus, and suggestions on how to include family recipes. The chapter closes by exploring different cuisines for inspiration. "A Couple's Story" features Jane and Sachin: A Wedding with Indian and Irish elements.

Chapter 16: To Taste Abundance: The Wedding Cake

The wedding cake or bread is used worldwide to encourage fertility, wish the couple a sweet life, and offer a taste of the abundance a marriage will produce.

The chapter focuses on traditional cakes by culture, helping the couple design one that represents their style and personality. The use of charms, trinkets, and ribbons is discussed along with selecting a filling and including a cake topper. The chapter concludes with the groom's cake.

Insert 5: Rosemary for Remembrance: Herbs

The final special insert focuses on the age-old tradition of wedding herbs. Herbal significance and symbolism along with dozens of suggestions for incorporating herbs into the wedding are highlighted. Design suggestions include herbal rings for votives, wine glasses and candles, herbal ribbons and ties, centerpieces, bouquets, boutonnieres, favors, and tosses.

Chapter 17: Dancing on the Embers: Reception Customs

At Belgian wedding celebrations, the bride and groom symbolically toss their past life onto the embers of a dying fire.

The chapter identifies reception traditions from around the world. Highlights include toasts, the sharing of food and drink, and customs that honor family and ancestors. "A Couple's Story" features Narelle and Jacopo: A Wedding with Australian, Italian, and Jamaican elements.

Chapter 18: Bringing the Wedding Vision to Life

The final chapter offers guidance for pulling all the elements together and provides organizational steps, resources, and design forms to complete the process.

Sample Chapter(s)

Sample Author-Agent Contract

Disclaimer: Please note the author wrote this contract based on several samples and you should seek legal advice on determining what to include in your contract. This should not serve to be the exact contract you plan to use.

LITERARY SERVICES, LLC ("Agent"), and Ima Author ("Author"), agree as follows:

GENERAL TERMS.

    1.1 Agent's Business. Agent is in the business of representing and promoting authors and providing other literary services for authors who are working in (or aspire to work in) the professional literary world.

    1.2 Author's Work. Agent shall have the exclusive right to negotiate for the disposition of literary rights for Author's work Name Of Book, subject to this Agreement. Author is the sole owner of all of the literary rights related to Author's Work (hereinafter referred to as "Literary Rights").

For the purpose of this Agreement, the term "Literary Rights" shall mean all of the literary and other intellectual property rights of every kind and nature whatsoever related to or derived from Author's creation of Author's Work, including without limitation all publishing rights, motion picture rights, audio rights, electronic rights, and merchandising rights both within the United States and everywhere else in the world (sometimes referred to as "Foreign Rights").

1.3 Engagement of Agent's Services. Author hereby engages Agent (and Agent's individual literary agent, Iman Agent), and Agent hereby accepts such engagement, as the exclusive professional literary agent of and for Author and as the promoter of Author's Work and of Author's literary career as a writer in the professional literary world ("Author's Literary Career"); provided, however, the term "Author's Literary Career" shall not include any of Author's work as a professional consultant, and Agent shall not be entitled to any compensation as a result of any income earned by Author from her work as a professional consultant.

1.4 Independent Contractor Relationship. Each of Agent and Author shall be deemed an independent contractor and neither shall be deemed to be the employee of the other, i.e., nothing in this Agreement shall be deemed to create an employee/employer, partnership, or joint venture relationship between Agent and Author.

1.5 Term. The term of this Agreement shall commence upon the signing of this Agreement by Agent and Author and shall continue unless terminated as provided in Paragraph 6.10 below.

1.6 Territory. The territory governed by this Agreement shall be worldwide.

2. PAYMENT TO AGENT, COMPENSATION OF AGENT, REIMBURSE-
MENT OF AGENT'S EXPENSES, REMITTANCE TO AUTHOR, AND
INSPECTION OF AGENT'S BOOKS. Except as otherwise provided in
this Agreement:

2.1 Payment to Agent. All gross receipts owed to Author by any
third-party, including without limitation any publisher or distrib-
utor, arising out of, derived from, or related in any way to the
sale or other disposition (during the term of this Agreement)
of any of Author's Literary Work and/or Literary Rights ("Author's Gross Receipts") shall be paid directly to Agent; and, for
this limited purpose, Author hereby appoints Agent as Author's
limited attorney-in-fact;

2.2 Agent's Compensation and Reimbursement of Expenses. In
consideration for Agent's performance of Agent's duties under
this Agreement:

2.2.1 Basic Agency Fee. As Agent's basic agency fee, Agent shall
be entitled to receive a total of fifteen percent (15%) of all
of Author's Gross Receipts (net of any sales tax or gross
receipts tax Author is liable for relative to such Author's
Gross Receipts) ("Agent's Basic Agency Fee"); provided,
however, Agent shall not be entitled to receive any commission or other sum with respect to any of Author's
Gross Receipts arising out of, derived from, or related to
any prior or pre-existing agreements between Author and
any third-party; AND

2.2.2 Additional Sub-Agency Fee. Upon subsequent written
agreement between Author and Agent, if Agent retains any
co-agent or sub-agent with respect to the commercializa-
tion and/or exploitation of any Foreign Rights with respect
to Author's Work and/or Literary Rights, Agent shall be
entitled to receive an additional ten percent (10%) of all of
Author's Gross Receipts derived from such Foreign Rights
("Agent's Additional Sub-Agency Fee"); provided, however,
except as specifically provided in this Paragraph 2.2.2 and
in Paragraph 2.2.3 (relating to Reimbursement of Agent's

Expenses) below, Agent shall be solely responsible for all payments made and/or owed to any other sub-agent and/or co-agents retained by Agent; AND

2.2.3 Reimbursement of Agent's Expenses. When any of Author's Literary Work has been successfully sold in one or more of the markets (domestic and/or foreign) to which it has been submitted, Agent shall be entitled to reimbursement of the reasonable and customary costs, fees, and expenses incurred by Agent's with regard to Agent's representation of Author ("Agent's Reimbursable Expenses"). Agent's Reimbursable Expenses shall include international mail costs, courier service fees, photocopying, and the cost of books used for international submissions. Author's approval of any expenses not listed above shall be required. Agent's Reimbursable Expenses shall not include any of Agent's usual and customary office expenses, e.g., telephone, staff, etc., which will be Agent's sole responsibility.

2.2.4 Effect of Sale of Rights after Termination of Agreement. If Author sells or transfers any Literary Rights in any of Author's Literary Work to any person or other entity to which Agent submitted a proposal for the sale of those rights during the term of this Agreement, Agent shall be entitled to the same compensation, i.e., Agent's Basic Agency Fee and any applicable Agent's Additional Sub-Agency Fee, and to reimbursement of Agent's Reimbursable Expenses if such sale or transfer of Literary Rights takes place within ninety (90) days after this Agreement terminates. Once earned under this Agreement, Agent's right to be compensated for any sale or disposition of Literary Rights in any of Author's Work shall continue even after this Agreement terminates.

2.3 Remittance to Author. Within ten (10) business days after Agent receives any of Author's Gross Receipts, Agent shall pay Author all sums collected as Author's Gross Receipts less only: (i) Agent's Basic Agency fee; (ii) any applicable Agent's Additional Sub-Agency Fee; and (iii) Agent's Reimbursable Expenses. At that time Agent shall also provide Author with an accounting (with reasonable supporting documentation) reflecting Author's Gross Receipts actually collected by Agent and an itemization of all deductions for: (i) Agent's Basic Agency Fee; (ii) any applicable Agent's Additional Sub-Agency Fee; and (iii) Agent's Reimbursable Expenses.

Except as otherwise provided in this Agreement, all sums paid to Agent under this Agreement shall be deemed to have been paid irrevocably.

2.4 Inspection of Books. Upon written request, Author and/or Author's representative shall have the right to examine Agent's books and records to the extent that such books and records pertain to any matters under this Agreement. Such examinations shall occur not more frequently than quarterly in any calendar year and shall be conducted at Agent's offices during normal business hours and at a mutually agreeable time. In order to mitigate the costs of such examination, within thirty (30) days after Author's written request to Agent, Agent shall provide to Author (or to Author's representative) photocopies or electronic copies (readable by standard office software) of all relevant records which could be examined by Author (or Author's representative) at Agent's offices pursuant to this paragraph.

3. DUTIES AND POWERS OF AGENT. During the term of this Agreement and subject to all other terms and conditions set forth in this Agreement:

3.1 Reasonable Best Efforts Performance. Agent shall render and perform Agent's professional literary agency and promotional services required under this Agreement on a "reasonable best efforts" basis. For the purpose of this Agreement, the term "reasonable best efforts" shall mean: (i) in a manner reasonably consistent with the generally accepted standards of care, quality, skill, and diligence generally applicable to the nature of Agent's professional services within the field of professional literary agents; and (ii) in a manner reasonably consistent with Agent's responsibilities to Agent's other clients, i.e., to Agent's other professional writers who are working in (or aspire to work in) the professional literary world; and (iii) in a manner reasonably likely to enhance Author's opportunities (given Author's individual and specific strengths, skills, vulnerabilities, and challenges) to succeed as a professional writer in the professional literary world.

3.2 Agent's Duties Relative to Literary Agency and Promotion of Author's Professional Career. Contingent upon Author's compliance with the terms and conditions of this Agreement, Agent shall:

3.2.1 Attempt to find appropriate publishers for Author's Work;

3.2.2 Negotiate on Author's behalf appropriate contracts with publishers for the publication of Author's Work and/or with other third-parties for the sale or other disposition of Author's Literary Rights relative to Author's Work throughout the world; provided, however, Author reserves final control over any agreement disposing of Author's Literary Rights, and no agreement disposing of any of Author's Literary Rights shall be binding without Author's signature.

3.2.3 Coach and assist Author with respect to the promotion of Author's Literary Career;

3.2.4 Consult with Author periodically as necessary or appropriate to maintain effective communication between Agent and Author with respect to Author's Literary Career;

3.2.5 Discuss with Author all enquiries from third-parties related to Author's Work and with regard to Author's Literary Career;

3.2.6 Provide Author with periodic reports of Agent's work and Agent's plans for future work for and on behalf of Author's Literary Career;

3.2.7 Assist Author with Author's collection of all monies owed to Author by third-parties with regard to Author's Work and with regard to Author's activities within Author's Literary Career, including without limitation all royalties due from publishers and other third-parties;

3.2.8 Provide Author with regular written reports setting forth relevant details relative to Agent's Reimbursable Expenses that are related solely to Agent's activities as Author's Agent and not as Agent of other Authors;

3.2.9 Maintain an account for all funds collected by Agent on Author's behalf; provided that such account may also hold funds collected by Agent on behalf of other clients of Agent; provided further, except to the extent of funds that are then owed to Agent by Author (or, with respect to funds collected by Agent on behalf of Agent's other clients, are then owed to Agent by such other clients of Agent), such account shall not hold Agent's funds, i.e., except to the extent of funds that are then owed to Agent, at all times all funds owed to Author shall be kept separate from and shall not be commingled with Agent's own operating funds.

4. NOTICES.

4.1 Manner of Notice. All notices which are required to be given under this Agreement or which either party desires to give to the other relative to any matter under this Agreement shall be in writing and (i) delivered personally to the other party or to any officer, director, or other agent or representative of the other party designated by such other party as having authority to receive such notices, or (ii) transmitted to the other party by facsimile or other electronic transmission, or (iii) delivered by a recognized overnight or two-day delivery service such as DHL or FedEx, or (iv) transmitted to the other party by electronic mail; provided, however, that any notice transmitted by facsimile or other electronic transmission or by electronic mail shall be followed up by personal delivery or overnight delivery within forty-eight (48) hours after the termination.

4.2 Notices to Agent. Any notice to Agent shall be sent to Agent at the following address/fax number/e-mail address, or to such other address/fax number/e-mail address as Agent may hereafter designate:

AGENT: Iman Agent, (address)

4.3 Notices to Author. Any notice to Author shall be sent to Author at the following address/fax number/e-mail address, or to such other address/fax number/e-mail address as Author may hereafter designate:

AUTHOR: Ima Author, (address)

4.4 Effective Date. Except as otherwise provided herein, the effective date of any notice hereunder shall be the earlier of the date such notice is actually delivered personally, or the date such notice is transmitted by facsimile or other electronic transmission, or the third day after the date such notice is deposited with a recognized overnight delivery service with the delivery charges prepaid.

5. DISPUTE RESOLUTION. In the event of any dispute between the parties, the parties shall attempt to resolve such disputes through discussion. If the parties are unable to resolve the disagreement, the parties agree to submit the disagreement to binding arbitration before a single arbitrator chosen by the parties. If the parties are unable to agree on an arbitrator, each party shall appoint a representative and the representatives shall choose a single arbitrator. The parties shall arbitrate the disagreement in accordance with and pursuant to the then existing rules of the American Arbitration Association. The parties also agree that an arbitrator may award reasonable costs and attorney fees to the winning party, and that the arbitration award may be enforced in any court with jurisdiction.

6. MISCELLANEOUS PROVISIONS.

6.1 Binding. This Agreement shall be binding up and shall inure to the benefit of the parties, their heirs, representatives, and assignees.

6.2 Time Is of The Essence. Time is of the essence as to all matters set forth in this Agreement. The failure of any party hereto to perform any obligation by the date required shall constitute a material and substantial breach of this Agreement.

6.3 Governing Law and Jurisdiction. This Agreement shall be governed in accordance with the laws of the State of IDAHO. The parties consent to the exclusive jurisdiction and venue of the federal and state courts located in Bonner County, Idaho, in any action arising out of or relating to this Agreement. The parties waive any other venue to which either party might be entitled by domicile or otherwise. The provisions of this paragraph shall not be construed or interpreted to conflict with the provisions of Paragraph 6.4 above, i.e., except for non-arbitral matters, if any, the parties shall be obligated to arbitrate any dispute arising under this Agreement.

6.4 Entire Agreement. This Agreement represents the entire agreement between Agent and Author relative to the subject matter of this Agreement and supersedes all prior negotiations, representations, and agreements relative to such subject matter.

6.5 Independent Provisions. Each of the provisions of this Agreement is independent of every other provision. In the event that any provision of this Agreement is determined to be invalid or unenforceable for any reason, the remaining provisions shall continue to be binding, valid, and effective with the invalid or unenforceable provisions being stricken the same as if never written.

6.6 Captions. The captions herein are for convenience only and shall have no legal effect.

6.7 No Assignment by Agent. Without Author's prior written consent, Agent shall not assign any of its rights, powers, or duties under this Agreement; provided, however, Agent may assign its right to receive compensation and reimbursement of Agent's Reimbursable Expenses to any third-party; and provided further if Agent is no longer in existence or actively involved in the business of (or operating within the field of) literary agency, then, on written notice from Author to Agent (or Agent's representatives), Author may assume responsibility for collection of all sums owed to Author by any publisher or other third-party, and Author shall continue to have the obligation to pay Agent all sums owed to Agent under Paragraphs 2.2.1 through 2.2.3 above.

6.8 No Waiver. No term or condition of this Agreement may be waived except by a writing signed by the party entitled to the benefit thereof. No waiver shall be construed to apply to any further or future default.

6.9 Warranties, Representations, and Indemnification. Each party represents and warrants that he/she/it has the right to enter into this Agreement without impairing anyone else's rights, and that he/she/it shall not to make any commitment relative to Author's Work and Author's Literary Rights that would conflict with this Agreement. Each party shall defend, indemnify, and hold the other party harmless from and against every claim based on any alleged breach of the provisions of this paragraph.

6.10 Early Termination. Either Agent or Author may terminate this Agreement at any time upon thirty (30) days prior written notice to the other.

6.11 Independent Advice and Mutual Preparation. Each party acknowledges that: (i) he/she/it has been advised to seek independent legal and tax advice with regard to this Agreement; (ii) this document shall be deemed to have been drafted by both parties and that no presumptions shall be made against either party based on the actual drafting of this Agreement or any provision of this Agreement; and (iii) he/she/it is entering into this Agreement freely and voluntarily.

Author: _____

Agent: _____

Date: _____

Sample Revised Pages

ORIGINAL DRAFT:

Unwillingly, I moved forward as the officer prodded me after the electronic hum sounded; then the large steel door slid open. Once I was inside, the door went the other way and locked with a loud and ominous sound that echoed throughout the whole corrections facility. Finding more than 3 feet of space between me and the other inmates was impossible in the over-crowded cell. I was scared, but it did not register because I was numb; still hearing the police officer yelling in my ear while putting on the handcuffs and charging me with a felony crime.

Just a short while ago, I was asleep and dreaming in my bed unusually passed my normal waking hours. Yes, they were good dreams but not for long. At 8:45am my door was pounding with a thunder the likes of which I had never heard. It was so loud that I through the covers off and ran to the door thinking it was an emergency opening it quickly only to be grabbed, handcuffed and taken away in the squad car.

In the jail cell, I was in my light summer pajamas and bedroom slippers. Not exactly my preferred dress for incarceration. Most people think of their clothes as a fashion statement; right now I was just wishing for protection from the cold and danger. Just some blue jeans and a regular shirt would do. With what I had on now, one quick jerk in a struggle and my flimsy summer pajamas, thinner than a T-Shirt would just tear off as rags.

I was once rich and free, but no more. Now being in a jail cell with criminals and charged with a felony was the last thing I thought would ever happen to me. My one phone call did not get through. Emotions were no good now and self preservation was the only thought on my mind. Staying alive was my only focus.

REVISED DRAFT:

It seems only a short time ago I was asleep in my bed, still dreaming long past my normal waking hour. And they were good dreams, but not for long. At 8:45 a.m., someone pounded on my door with a thunder the likes of which I had never heard. It was so loud I thought it had to be an emergency. I threw the covers off, bolted out of bed, and ran to the door. As soon as I opened it I was grabbed, handcuffed, and shoved into a squad car.

An electronic hum sounded and a large steel door slid open. Unwillingly, I moved forward as the officer prodded. Once I was inside the door slammed shut behind me and locked with a loud and ominous sound that echoed throughout the corrections facility. Finding more than three feet of space between myself and the other inmates was impossible in the over-crowded cell. I was scared but it did not register. I was numb — still hearing the sound of the police officer yelling in my ear while he shackled my wrists and charged me with a felony.

In the jail cell I was still in my light summer pajamas and bedroom slippers. Not exactly my preferred dress for incarceration. Most people think of their clothes as a fashion statement; right now, I was just wishing for protection from the cold and danger. A pair of blue jeans and a regular shirt would do. With what I had on now, one quick jerk in a struggle and my flimsy summer pajamas, thinner than a well-worn T-shirt, would tear off in rags.

I was once rich and free, but no more. Being in a jail cell with criminals and charged with a felony was the last thing I thought would ever happen to me. My one phone call did not get through. Emotions were no good now and self-preservation was the only thought on my mind. Staying alive was my only focus.

Bibliography

Katz, Christina. *Get Known Before The Book Deal: Use Your Personal Strengths to Grow an Author Platform.* (Writer's Digest Books, 2008)

Larson, Michael. *How To Get A Literary Agent.* (Sourcebooks, Inc., 2006)

Larson, Michael. *How To Write a Book Proposal.* (Writer's Digest Books, 1997)

Lyon, Elizabeth. *The Sell Your Novel Tool Kit.* (Penguin Books, 1997)

Sambuchino, Chuck. *2009 Guide to Literary Agents.* (Writer's Digest Books, 2008)

Sinclair, Elizabeth. *The Dreaded Synopsis.* (Thomas Max Publishing, 2009)

About the Author

Laura Cross is a freelance editor, author, and screenwriter. She has ghost-written numerous books on various subjects and teaches nonfiction writing workshops. Her author-clients have appeared on Oprah, and been featured in *Publishers Weekly, The New York Times's* book review section, and on Amazon.com's[SM] bestseller list. Laura is the owner of Scenario Writing Studio where she specializes in developing compelling book proposals for her clients. Her blog, True Story Ink, offers tips on writing and marketing your nonfiction book. You may contact her at:

Laura Cross
Scenario Writing Studio
877.836.5850

Web site: **www.scenariowritingstudio.com**
Blog: **www.truestoryink.com**
E-mail: laura@scenariowitingstudio.com

Index

A

Action, 178, 180, 275, 187, 191-192, 29, 34, 36, 122

Advance, 201, 248, 17, 64, 121, 148, 157-160, 165

Adventure, 177-178, 180, 182, 36, 42, 82

Artwork, 201, 260, 18

Author's Voice or Author's style, 201

B

Back cover, 201, 19

Beta readers, 117, 119

Biography, 174, 177-181, 183, 249, 251-252, 42, 63

Book dealer, 201

Book distribution, 201

Book reviewer, 201

C

Cooking, 175, 40, 82, 100, 104

Copy editing, 201, 18

Copyeditors, 118

Copyright, 201-202, 18, 20, 123

Credentials, 202, 24, 30, 45-46, 50, 55, 84, 89-90, 103, 106, 126-127, 153

Crime, 175, 178, 181, 279, 183-185, 188, 190-194, 34-35, 38, 43, 83, 90, 115, 125, 137

Critique Groups, 117, 119

D

Digital publishing, 16, 19

Dust jacket, 202

E

Endorsement, 202

Exclusive, 267-268, 275, 202, 72, 149

F

Fantasy, 173-175, 178-179, 181, 212, 184, 187-194, 34-36, 38, 51, 65, 92, 115, 137, 144, 168

Film rights, 202, 204, 17, 22, 144

Food, 177-181, 234, 183, 247, 257, 264-265, 40, 77, 100

Foreign rights, 268-269, 202, 22, 63, 145

Foreword, 202, 17, 87, 9

G

Galleys, 202, 150

H

Horror, 178, 183, 187-194, 32, 34, 37, 79, 113, 168

I

Imprint, 202

Inspirational, 178, 207, 197, 36, 38, 40, 42, 139, 10

Interior layout, 202, 19

ISBN (International Standard Book Number), 202, 18

L

Library of Congress Catalog Number, 202

M

Marketing department, 203, 19, 101, 113

Memoir, 173-181, 207, 184, 190, 43, 65-66, 78, 95

Metaphysical, 40

Multiple submissions, 203, 93

Mystery, 174-178, 181, 212-213, 232, 237, 184, 187-194, 34-36, 38, 85, 93, 115, 125, 137

O

One-Time Rights, 203

Option clause, 203, 164

P

Popular trend, 203, 31, 86

Portfolio, 211, 223, 198, 204, 248, 255, 49-51, 104

Potential sales, 203, 31, 100

Print on demand (POD), 203

Promotional Plan, 203, 25, 97, 101, 107

Proofreader, 118

Publishing contracts, 21

R

Religious, 175, 178, 192, 196, 253-254, 34-36, 38, 40

Reprint Rights, 203, 161

Royalties, 273, 203, 21-22, 91, 145, 150, 160-161

Royalty payments, 160-161

S

Science Fiction, 184, 188-193, 35-36, 38

Seasonal publishing, 32

Self-help, 174-179, 181, 32, 38-39, 85, 88, 137, 139

Self-publishing, 203, 16-17, 19

Serial Rights, 204, 22, 145, 161

Simultaneous submission, 204

Solicited, 204, 136

Subsidiary rights, 203-204, 15-16, 22, 28-29, 62-63, 91, 144-145, 149, 151, 160-161, 164, 168

Suspense, 175, 177-178, 181, 188-193, 197, 34-35, 38, 89, 111, 125-126, 137

T

Thriller, 176-178, 181, 183, 187-193, 33-36, 38, 83, 89, 111, 137

Timely and relevant, 204, 31

Titles, 202, 204, 18, 22, 76, 79, 85-86, 92, 99-101, 106

Travel Guides, 38-39

True crime, 175, 178, 43, 83, 125

Typeface, 204

U

University Press, 204, 17

W

Westerns, 178, 35-36

Women's Fiction, 173-181, 197, 37-38, 125, 168

Y

Young Adult, 237, 194, 29, 34-35, 37-38